Brilliant guides

C000157494

What you need to know and how to do it

When you're working on your computer and come up against a problem that you're unsure how to solve, or want to accomplish something in an application that you aren't sure how to do, where do you look? Manuals and traditional training guides are usually too big and unwieldy and are intended to be used as end-to-end training resources, making it hard to get to the info you need right away without having to wade through pages of background information that you just don't need at that moment – and helplines are rarely that helpful!

Brilliant guides have been developed to allow you to find the info you need easily and without fuss and guide you through the task using a highly visual, step-by-step approach – providing exactly what you need to know when you need it!

Brilliant guides provide the quick easy-to-access information that you need, using a table of contents and troubleshooting guide to help you find exactly what you need to know, and then presenting each task in a visual manner. Numbered steps guide you through each task or problem, using numerous screenshots to illustrate each step. Added features include 'See also...' boxes that point you to related tasks and information in the book, while 'Did you know?...' sections alert you to relevant expert tips, tricks and advice to further expand your skills and knowledge.

In addition to covering all major office PC applications, and related computing subjects, the *Brilliant* series also contains titles that will help you in every aspect of your working life, such as writing the perfect CV, answering the toughest interview questions and moving on in your career.

Brilliant guides are the light at the end of the tunnel when you are faced with any minor or major task.

Publisher's acknowledgements

The author and publisher would like to thank the following for permission to reproduce the material in this book:

Mozilla Corp., FastMail Pty. Ltd, CyberLink Corp., Nullsoft Inc., WinZip International LLC., Live365 Inc., VLCPlayer.com, Zone Labs LLC., Lavasoft, GRISOFT s.r.o., CNETdownload.com, Fresh Communications Ltd, More2 Ltd, Advanced Micro Devices Inc., Kingston, Creative Technology Ltd, Plextor Corp. and John Taylor.

Microsoft product screen shot(s) reprinted with permission from Microsoft Corporation.

Every effort has been made to obtain necessary permission with reference to copyright material. The publisher apologises if, inadvertently, any sources remain unacknowledged and will be glad to make the necessary arrangements at the earliest opportunity.

Author's acknowledgements

The author would like to thank Paul Lester, Angela Orchard, Dom Brookman, Sally Mortimore and Karen Mosman for their assistance.

About the author

Matt Powell is a technical editor at Imagine Publishing. He has written for a wide variety of computing and technology magazines including *PC Home*, *GigaHz*, *Windows XP Made Easy*, *Advanced Photoshop*, *PC Basics*, *eBuyer*, *Internet User*, *Digital Camera Buyer* and *PC First Aid*.

Contents

Introduction

Welcome to *Brilliant Microsoft® Vista Computer Basics*, a visual quick-reference book that gives you a basic grounding in the way computers work, introduces the Windows operating system and demonstrates how to use common applications – a complete reference for the beginner user.

Find what you need to know – when you need it

You don't have to read this book in any particular order. We've designed the book so that you can jump in, get the information you need, and jump out. To find the information that you need, just look up the task in the table of contents or Troubleshooting guide, and turn to the page listed. Read the task introduction, follow the step-by-step instructions along with the illustration along with the illustration, and you're done.

How this book works

Each task is presented with step-by-step instructions in one column and screen illustrations in the other. This arrangement lets you focus on a single task without having to turn the pages too often.

How you'll learn

Find what you need to know – when you need it

How this book works

Step-by-step instructions

Troubleshooting guide

Spelling

Step-by-step instructions

This book provides concise step-by-step instructions that show you how to accomplish a task. Each set of instructions includes illustrations that directly correspond to the easy-to-read steps. Eye-catching text features provide additional helpful information in bite-sized chunks to help you work more efficiently or to teach you more in-depth information. The 'For your information' feature provides tips and techniques to help you work smarter, while the 'See also' cross-references lead you to other parts of the book containing related information about the task. Essential information is highlighted in 'Important' boxes that will ensure you don't miss any vital suggestions and advice.

Troubleshooting guide

This book offers quick and easy ways to diagnose and solve common problems that you might encounter, using the Troubleshooting guide. The problems are grouped into categories that are presented alphabetically.

Spelling

We have used UK spelling conventions throughout this book. You may therefore notice some inconsistencies between the text and the software on your computer which is likely to have been developed in the USA. We have however adopted US spelling for the words 'disk' and 'program' as these are becoming commonly accepted throughout the world.

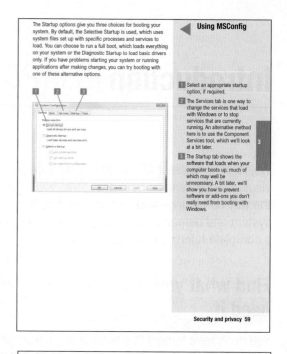

The Startup options give you three choices for booting your system. By default, the Selective Startup is used, which uses system files set up with specific processes and services to load. You can choose to run a full boot, which loads everything on your system or the Diagnostic Startup to load basic drivers only. If you have problems starting your system or running applications after making changes, you can try booting with one of these alternative options.

Using MSConfig

1 Select an appropriate startup option, if required.

2 The Services tab is one way to change the services that load with Windows or to stop services that are currently running. An alternative method here is to use the Component Services tool, which we'll look at a bit later.

3 The Startup tab shows the software that loads when your computer boots up, much of which may well be unnecessary. A bit later, we'll show you how to prevent software or add-ons you don't really need from booting with Windows.

Security and privacy 59

Troubleshooting guide

Introducing your PC

Introduction

Before we focus on software applications and how to actually use your computer to accomplish things, we're going to take a peek inside a PC to discover what exactly it is each part does. Although this may be the last thing you want to do right now, a little knowledge about the innards of your computer can go a long way once you've mastered the operating system and software applications. Many minor problems can be fixed with a little hardware maintenance and all it takes will be a screwdriver and perhaps a touch of elbow grease. There's absolutely no soldering, welding or hardware engineering involved! It can be a little scary the first time you pop open the case and see bundles of wires and mysterious slabs of silicon, but today's systems are modular and designed to be as simple as possible. Unless you ignore a few basic safety rules, it's very difficult to hurt either yourself or your PC. The most important of these is a no-brainer: always switch off the power to your system before opening the case. Shut the system down and then flick the power switch on the back of your power supply unit to ensure there's no chance it'll power up. You can safely leave it plugged in once the power supply unit (PSU) is off and in fact this is recommended as it will keep your PC grounded. Static is the PC enthusiasts worst enemy and will fry the most delicate (and expensive) parts in the blink of an eye. Try not to perform maintenance while standing on carpet or any other material that easily builds static and always touch a grounded metal object beforehand to discharge any build-up. You can also buy anti-static wristbands for a few pounds from any good PC store – they clip onto a metal surface and keep static from building. Magnetism and electronics don't mix either, so

What you'll do

Motherboard

Central Processing Unit

Random Access Memory

Hard disk drive

Graphics card

Sound card

Optical drive

Floppy disk drive

Power supply unit

PC case

> **!**
> ### Important
> Always switch off the power to your system before opening the case.

make sure you have a screwdriver with non-magnetic head and don't slap fridge magnets onto the side of your case! If you're going to poke about regularly inside computers it's not a bad idea to purchase a proper PC toolkit, which will usually contain a screwdriver with the correct heads, anti-static wristband and many other useful extras. The final important safety tip is never to apply excessive force to any component. If you're trying to remove something and it's not budging, take your time, check for well-hidden catches, levers or screws and carefully try to work it out. The last thing you want to do is damage your graphics card or motherboard because you forgot about the catch holding it in place on the expansion slot.

Think of the motherboard as your PC's central nervous system. Its job is to connect and manage each component, shuttling data to the correct location. Not all motherboards are the same and the type of hardware you can use is restricted by what will physically fit on the board and what is supported by the motherboard chipset.

Central Processing Unit

Continuing the biological analogy, the central processing unit (usually referred to as the CPU or processor) is your PC's brain. It does the hard work of calculating and sorting all the data going through your system. The power of a modern CPU is measured in Gigahertz (GHz), while older CPUs were measured in Megahertz (MHz). The GHz number is becoming less relevant however, particularly with the latest dual-core processors. A dual-core CPU contains two physical processors, meaning it's capable of handling several tasks at once without slowing down your system.

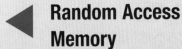

Random Access Memory (RAM), or just memory, is extremely fast volatile memory that provides temporary data storage when a computer is in use. Volatile memory loses the data held when there's no power. The more RAM you have, the faster your system will operate as it's able to shunt data there while getting on with other tasks and then retrieve it when needed. RAM often comes in pairs, but since there are many different kinds of RAM these must be of the same type and, preferably, from the same manufacturer.

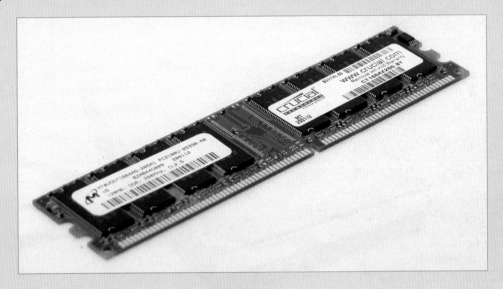

Hard disk drive

The hard disk, also known as a hard drive or HDD, is the main storage medium for modern computer systems. While RAM is volatile, hard disks are non-volatile so data stored there remains even when there is no power. Current consumer-level hard disks have reached a massive 750 gigabytes (Gb) in capacity, enough for many thousands of movies, music and image files. Hard disks use two different types of interface to connect to your computer, either IDE or the newer SATA.

The graphics card provides the vital function of processing and outputting visuals to your monitor. Some motherboards include graphics chips built onto them but dedicated Graphics Processing Units (GPUs) offer hugely superior performance and save the CPU from having to handle graphics in addition to other tasks. Gamers demand expensive, high-end graphics cards but they're not necessary for standard Windows applications.

Sound card

Sound cards allow you to play music through your PC. The majority of motherboards now include integrated sound chipsets which are perfectly suitable for music, games and videos, but musicians and dedicated gamers prefer separate expansion cards which offer superior audio quality, a wider range of features and a greater selection of inputs and outputs for specialist equipment.

An optical drive gives you the capability to read and write CD and DVD discs. At a bare minimum you'll need a DVD reader to install software and perhaps play DVD video discs but DVD writers, or burners as they are also known, are now so cheap there's no reason not to own one since they offer an easy and affordable backup system. When buying a DVD writer you should check that it supports both + and – discs and also dual-layer DVDs.

Floppy disk drive

The floppy drive, or FDD, has long since been superseded by CD and DVD drives but may still be useful to some who need to read old 3.5-inch floppy disks. They're so inexpensive that it makes sense to have one just in case.

Power supply unit

The Power supply unit (PSU) supplies and regulates power to your PC. The output of a PSU, measured in watts, is important as this limits how much hardware you can add to your system before the power requirements exceed the capability of your PSU. For most of us a good quality, brand-name 400W power supply is perfectly adequate.

PC case

Usually referred to as the case, enclosure, or chassis, this metal or plastic box is what holds all your components together. Cases vary in price and complexity from sub-£20 plastic models to high-tech aluminium costing many hundreds of pounds. If you have a choice it is worth looking at your options, since airflow, build quality and features can be important depending on your needs. If you're running a system with expensive high-end graphics cards and hard disks you'll need to ensure that there's a constant flow of cool air. You may also want extras such as tool-less operation, which allows you to open the case and remove components without a screwdriver, or accessible front-mounted interface ports.

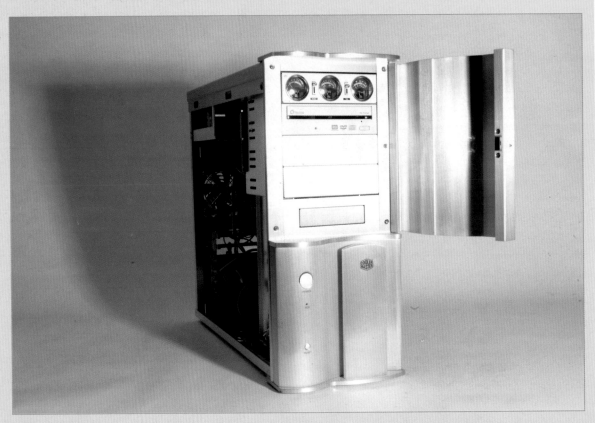

Welcome to Windows Vista

2

Introduction

On 30 January 2007 Microsoft launched the newest iteration of Windows. Windows Vista is the largest overhaul to the Windows operating system since Windows 95 and introduces a slew of new features and improvements, the most noticeable change being a smooth new interface dubbed 'Aero'. It is still recognisably Windows, though if you're a newcomer to Vista it can be a confusing experience at first. There are myriad options hidden away beneath sub-menus and some of Vista's security features can seem overly restrictive. Experienced XP users may even have more trouble than total novices to begin with since many familiar settings and menus have moved elsewhere.

To complicate matters even further there are several versions of Vista each offering an increasing number of features. For home users there is Home Basic, Home Premium and Ultimate. Home Basic, as the name suggests, is the cheapest edition and only offers the minimum you need. The major security enhancements are present along with a new version of Internet Explorer but it does not include the Aero interface. Home Premium has everything included in Basic plus the Aero user interface, Windows Media Center, DVD Maker application and support for playing DVD movies. Ultimate contains everything found in Basic and Premium plus the new BitLocker drive encryption and Volume Shadow Copy, which takes snapshots of your system and allows you to retrieve previous versions of files. This is the most expensive version however, costing, at the time of writing, over £300, so we'd recommend Home Premium for most users as it strikes a good balance between price and features.

We're going to start off with the basics – how to manage the icons on your desktop. Although your desktop will be empty initially, it's not going to be long before you've filled it with files and program shortcuts. Not only can it become difficult to find what you're looking for, but performance can be affected as Windows struggles to update all the icon graphics each time it loads. The occasional spot of housekeeping will also make your PC look far more organised.

Moving and arranging icons on the desktop

Move icons

1 Click on an icon, hold the mouse button and drag it to where you want it to go.

2 Groups of icons can be moved by clicking and holding on an empty part of the desktop and dragging a selection box over them. Release the mouse then click and hold on any one of the selected icons to move all of them.

Did you know?

Any icons on your computer can be moved and arranged in the same manner as desktop icons. Anywhere in Windows you can select icons and drag and drop to move them to different folders or locations, or arrange them using the context menu.

Jargon buster

Icon – graphical representation of a file or other object. They usually indicate what type of file the item is but can be customised by the user.

Shortcut – link to another location on your computer. If you want to run an application, they save you from navigating to the directory where that program is stored.

Moving and arranging icons on the desktop (cont.)

Arrange icons

1. You can have Windows arrange icons by right-clicking on an empty area of the desktop to bring up the context menu, then open the View menu and choose Auto Arrange.

2. You can choose the order in which they are arranged by opening the Sort By submenu and selecting Name, Size, Type or Date.

3. If you wish to place the icons anywhere on the desktop, disable both Auto Arrange and Snap To Grid options.

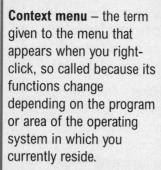

Jargon buster

Context menu – the term given to the menu that appears when you right-click, so called because its functions change depending on the program or area of the operating system in which you currently reside.

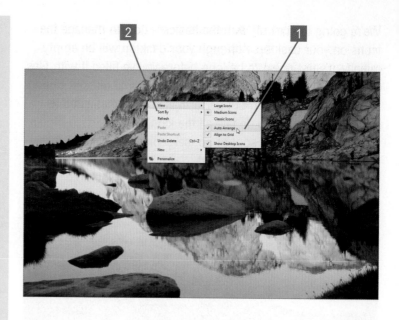

Timesaver tip

You can use shortcut keys to grab icons. Hold down Shift then click once on the first and last icons in a group you want to select and they will all be highlighted. Holding down Ctrl allows you to select one icon at a time, for example, choosing every other icon in a row. Combine these two by using Shift to select a group, releasing it, then selecting others or removing those already chosen by holding down Ctrl and clicking once on any you don't want selected.

The Sidebar is a brand new feature in Windows Vista. A pane on the side of your desktop provides quick access to calendars, system information and the latest news with the use of mini-applications known as gadgets. A few are included with Vista but you can download many thousands more from the Microsoft website.

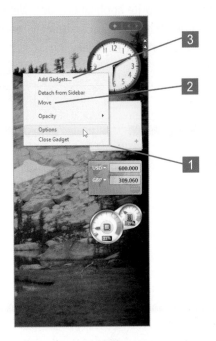

1 Right-click on a gadget to close, move or access options when they are available.

2 Click and hold this button to reposition the gadget on the Sidebar or detach it and drag to the desktop.

3 To enable more gadgets, choose Add Gadgets from the context menu.

4 Double-click on a gadget to add it to the Sidebar.

5 Click a gadget to view a description.

6 Visit Microsoft's gadget download site by clicking the Get more gadgets link.

7 Search all installed gadgets.

Using the taskbar

The taskbar is that bar that stretches the entire width of your screen with the Start Menu to the left and system tray to the right. When you open a program, it appears in the taskbar and can be minimized or bought back into focus by clicking once. Simple! You do have some additional options for customisation though, which can make it much easier to get access to your favourite applications and websites. Additional toolbars can be added or you can quickly rearrange program windows and folders for easy viewing.

Arrange program and folder windows

1 Right-click on an empty section of the taskbar and choose Cascade, Stacked or Side by Side from the context menu to automatically align the visible windows.

2 Use Undo to reverse the window alignment you've just set.

3 Click Show the Desktop to minimize all windows and reveal the desktop.

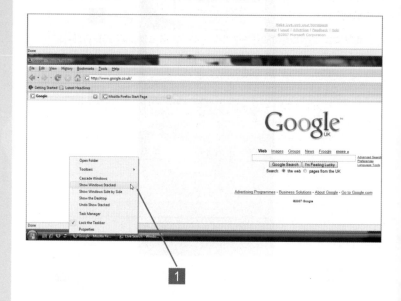

Timesaver tip

Hold Alt and press Tab to bring up a menu that allows you to move quickly between all windows on the taskbar. Keep tapping Tab until the window you want is selected then release both keys to bring it into focus. Vista Premium and Ultimate users also have an alternative method when using the Aero interface. Instead of Alt+Tab, try pressing the Windows Key and Tab to bring up the new 'Flip 3D' feature, which uses a 3D menu to show large, dynamic previews of your open windows.

Jargon buster

Folders – also called directories, are what Windows uses to organise all the files. Think of them like the filing cabinets in an office, a way of keeping relevant files grouped together for easy access.

System tray – the area to the far right of the taskbar. It is often used by applications to display status icons, while some programs have the option to minimize to the system tray rather than the taskbar.

Toolbars – groups of related options and tools, usually represented by icons. Toolbars can be floating in a program window or embedded into the top or side of an application window (sometimes called sidebars). Sidebars are often customisable, giving users the option to disable them or add and remove icons.

2

Configuring the taskbar

You can configure the taskbar through its Properties dialogue box. To open this, right-click on the taskbar and choose Properties.

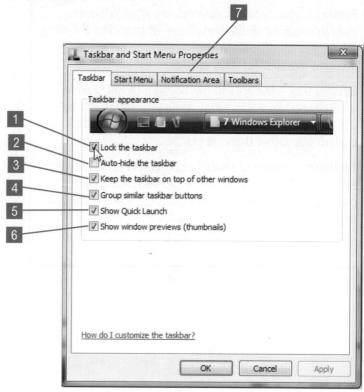

1 Lock and unlock the taskbar with the Lock the taskbar setting.

2 Auto-hide will cause the taskbar to slide out of view until you place the mouse cursor over it.

3 Disabling the option to keep the taskbar on top of other windows will hide it behind the current active folder or application.

4 With Group similar taskbar buttons enabled, buttons from the same application will be grouped when the taskbar is full.

5 Enabling Quick Launch places a row of useful shortcut icons to the left of the taskbar.

6 Show window previews is a new option that displays small thumbnail previews when you hover the mouse over a window in the taskbar.

7 Click the Notification Area tab to access settings related to the System Tray.

Important

Many programs place icons in the System Tray. Some are there when Windows starts, others when a program is run. They can provide useful shortcuts to functions, but may not be essential to the operation of a program. Also, having too many running in the System Tray when Windows starts can slow down your PC. If you wish to disable System Tray icons, check the options and settings for applications that use it as they will usually allow you to remove them.

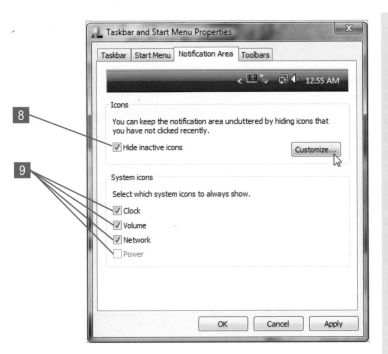

8 Check Hide inactive icons to automatically hide the icons you use the least. The Customise button next to it allows you to set the behaviour of individual icons.

9 You can choose to always show these particular icons on the taskbar by checking them from this list.

2

Adding toolbars to the taskbar

1 You can enable a pre-defined toolbar by right-clicking on the taskbar, opening the Toolbars menu and clicking one of those already listed. The same options can also be found in the Toolbars menu with the Taskbar Properties.

2 Add your own by choosing New Toolbar from the toolbars menu. Select any folder on your system.

3 If you start typing the name of folders and directories into the Folder text box, Windows will attempt to help you find the location you're typing by auto-filling the name.

4 Remove custom toolbars by going back to the Toolbars menu and clicking on the unwanted toolbar.

Important

On a fresh installation of Windows the language bar, which allows you to quickly switch languages, is enabled by default and placed to the right of the taskbar. You can disable this by right-clicking it and choosing Close. Take note of the message that appears telling you how to re-enable it via the Regional and Language Options settings.

Timesaver tip

Folders can also be dragged onto the taskbar to instantly make them into toolbars.

The Windows Start menu is where all your program shortcuts are stored; it allows you to get quick access to any installed applications (provided they've placed an icon there) plus various other tools like Search and Control Panel. It's also where you go to shut down, log-off or restart your computer. The Start menu is easy to manage as it's simply a folder on your PC that contains all the shortcuts, so you can drag and drop icons to it just as you would any other directory.

As with the rest of Windows, the Start menu is customisable and has bundles of options to play with. You have a choice of sticking with the default Windows Vista Start menu or switching to the Classic Start menu, which is essentially the same as that found in previous versions of Windows. The Start menu has received quite an overhaul in Vista so you may feel more comfortable using the Classic layout.

2

1 Click to put your PC in stand-by mode.

2 Lock your PC. To get back to your desktop you'll have to enter your password.

3 Open a submenu containing further options for turning off your PC or logging out of Windows.

4 Open the Windows Vista help application.

5 Use this option to change the applications that run when you access particular files.

6 Opens a submenu or new window showing the Control Panel, depending on whether you have chosen to open it as a menu or a link in the Start menu customisation options.

7 Connect to available networks.

8 View your local network.

Using the Start menu (cont.)

9 Access the drives and devices connected to your PC.

10 Opens a list of the most recently accessed files.

11 Quick access to the current user's folders – click the user icon to open the user account control panel.

12 These are pinned shortcuts which are always available.

13 This is a list of the most recent applications – right-click and choose the Pin to Start Menu option to have them permanently displayed.

14 Opens a menu showing all applications installed on your computer.

15 Search for an application.

Jargon buster

Control Panel – an important area of Windows that contains links to settings and controls for hardware, software and peripherals.

Quick Launch is a customisable shortcut bar that's enabled through the Start Menu properties. Applications will often place a shortcut here as well as on the desktop.

1 Click and drag icons onto the Quick Launch to make shortcuts. You can choose where the icon is placed before releasing the mouse button.

2 Move icons on Quick Launch by dragging and moving them to a different position.

3 Once you've filled up the space available to Quick Launch, icons will be moved to a pop-up window. Click the arrow to access them.

4 Use the Show Desktop icon to instantly minimise every program and reveal the desktop.

5 To increase the size of Quick Launch, unlock the taskbar by right-clicking on the taskbar and selecting Unlock, a bar will appear next to Quick Launch allowing you to extend its size.

Customising the Start menu

The Start menu is highly customisable, with bundles of options to enable extra functions or change the look completely. You have a choice of sticking with the default Start menu or switching to the Classic Start menu, which is essentially the same as that found in Windows 98, 2000 and Me. If you've used previous editions of Windows you may feel more comfortable with Classic, but the new Vista Start menu is much improved, with some helpful new features.

1 You can move icons around on the Start menu simply by clicking and dragging them to a new position, though it's much easier to organise by right-clicking on the Start button.

2 You can choose Explore, Open or Explore All Users from the Start menu context options. Explore is the easiest to use if you're moving icons.

3 Because the Start menu is just another folder on your system it works like any other directory within Windows. Grab folders or icons and drag them, or right-click to create a new shortcut or folder. Note that as every user account has its own Start menu, you can hide shortcuts from specific users by removing them from each personal Start menu folder or make them available to everyone by placing a link in the All Users folder.

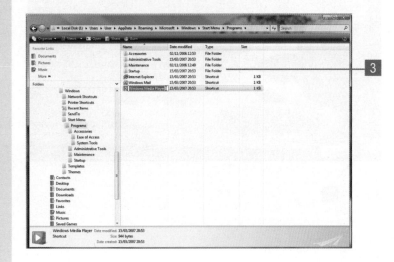

Timesaver tip

If you want to create a shortcut to a file or folder, hold down the right mouse button when you drag an icon instead of the left. When you release it, a menu will appear asking if you want to Copy, Move or Create a Shortcut. This is very helpful when you want to move instead of copying and vice versa, or create shortcuts in the Start menu or another location. Simply find the item you want to link, click and drag with the right mouse button and choose Create a Shortcut. If you hold the button while dragging and hover over the Start menu or a minimised window in the taskbar for a second, it will open as though you had clicked on it. You can do this through subfolders in the Start menu, releasing the button when you reach the desired location for the shortcut.

When adjusting the Start menu properties, selecting Classic over the default Start menu will change the look and behaviour of the menu drastically, removing the recently-accessed programs, pinned menu items and other new shortcuts and features found in Vista.

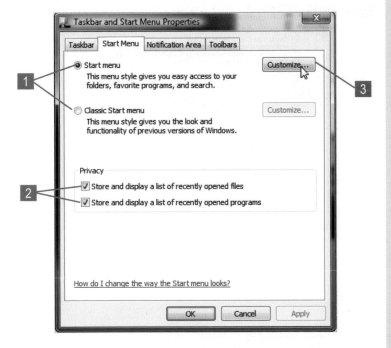

1 Right-click on the Start menu icon and click Properties. You can select either Start menu or Classic Start menu here – click the radio button next to either option then hit Apply.

2 Use these privacy options to choose whether or not you want Windows to keep track of recently accessed programs and files.

3 Click Customise next to either Start menu option to see further options relating to each.

Using Start menu properties (cont.)

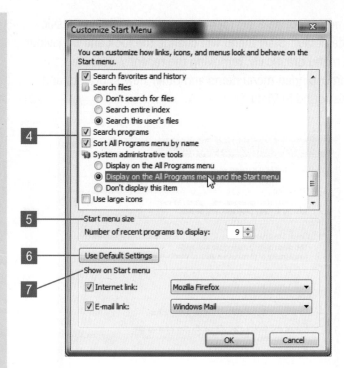

4 In the default Start menu you'll find a lengthy list of options for adjusting a wide range of features on your desktop. You can choose to enable or disable large desktop icons, remove some links from the Start menu or add new options, like re-enabling the 'Run' command.

5 Change this number to set the number of recent programs to be displayed on your Start menu.

6 Click this button to reset all options to their defaults.

7 Use these options to enable/disable Internet and email shortcuts and select the default web browser and email program.

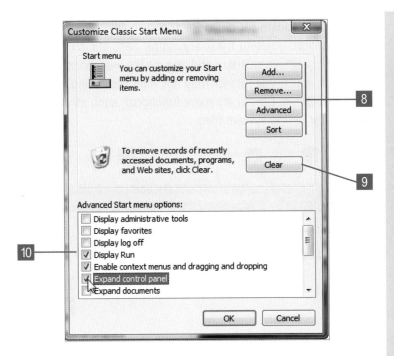

2

Customise the Classic Start menu

8 Click Add or Remove to manage Start Menu shortcuts through a wizard. The Advanced button opens up an Explorer window while Sort arranges icons into alphabetical order.

9 Press Clear to remove all records of recently accessed programs, files and websites

10 The advanced options let you expand the Control Panel and other folders of the Start menu so you don't need to open them to access a particular file or application.

Important

Each user account has its own Start menu configuration. If you wish to have a program available to every user on the system, make sure there is a shortcut in the 'All Users' Start menu folder. For more information on user accounts, see Chapter 3.

Creating and using folders

In Windows, folders (or directories) offer plenty of options for customisation. Some of these are simply aesthetic changes that add or remove sidebars and change the way icons are displayed, which you may or may not want depending on individual tastes. Others are more functional, such as the settings for hiding system files.

1. Create a new folder by bringing up the context menu with a right-click. Open the New submenu, choose Folder and enter a name. Folders can be created anywhere on your system.

2. In the address bar you can navigate up through subfolders by clicking on a folder name, or view all subfolders by clicking the arrow icons. You can also navigate directly to drives and folders by typing the address here.

3. Most options along this bar will change depending on the type of files within the current folder, apart from the Organise and Views menus.

4. Use Organise to add new panes and access folder options.

5. Click Views to change the layout of folder items.

6. The Folders and Favourite Links allow you to jump quickly to user folders and navigate the drives on your computer.

7. This preview appears when you select certain file types, including images and text files. It's enabled via the Organise menu.

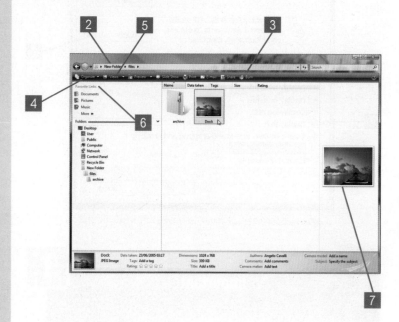

Jargon buster

File extension – indicates the type of file. The response when the file is opened depends upon the application with which it is associated. Windows will prompt the user to select an action when unrecognised files are accessed.

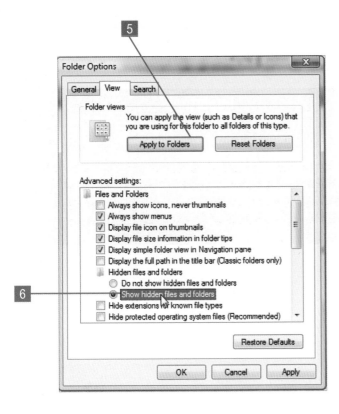

Changing folder options

1 To access folder options click Organise and then Folder and Search Options or, if the menu bar is enabled, click Tools then Folder Options.

2 Switch to Windows classic folders to disable the preview and filters features.

3 Set the Browse folders option to view folders in the existing window or open them in a new window.

4 The Click items option allows you to make icons behave like web links, so a single click will open them. This applies to all icons on your system.

5 In the View tab, click Apply to Folders to make the settings for the current folder universal.

6 By default, Windows hides system files and folders. In Advanced settings, you can make these visible. There are also other settings that change the way files are displayed.

Changing folder options (cont.)

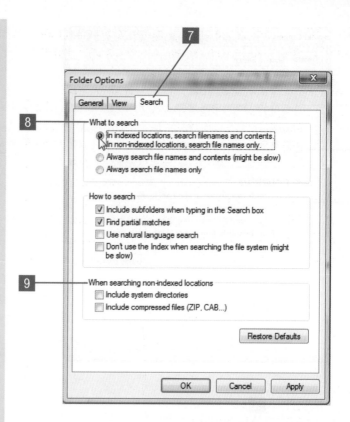

7 Within the Search tab you'll find options for adjusting the behaviour of Vista's powerful new search feature which indexes the files on your system, greatly reducing the time it takes to locate files.

8 By default Windows will only search the contents of files it has indexed. You can force it to look inside every file on your system but this will affect the speed.

9 Select whether the search will include compressed files and system directories, both of which can slow it down.

Important

Most applications will attempt to register themselves to handle certain file types when they're installed. If you install a new video player, for example, and don't want it to take over playing video files, make sure you check the installation options. Good programs ask before changing your file associations.

Windows offers a wide range of features for customising the look and feel of the OS to suit the needs of each user, whether you want to change the way it behaves or simply use an attractive desktop background. Using themes allows you to quickly apply matching colours, icons, fonts and sounds. There are also various settings for changing the general appearance and applying effects. If you have an older system, switching off the effects make Windows feel noticeably snappier. It's not just about aesthetics, though. There are a number of accessibility features that can assist those who have sight and hearing problems or difficulty typing. All these options are found in Windows Vista under the new Personalisation menu, which replaces the old desktop properties.

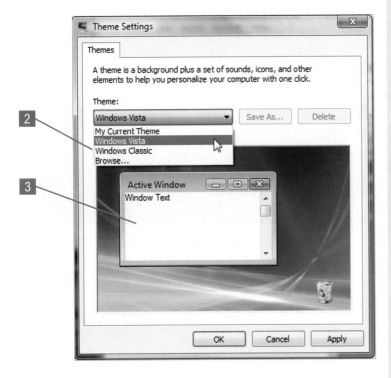

 Selecting a desktop theme

1 Right-click on a blank area of the desktop and click Personalise from the menu, then choose the Themes option.

2 The Themes tab allows you to manage Windows Vista themes. The default is 'Windows Vista' but you can also select Windows Classic, which makes Vista look like older versions of Windows.

3 This window will show a preview of the selected theme. Once you're happy, click Apply.

See also

Go to page 44 to learn how to configure the built-in accessibility options.

Choosing a desktop background

▶

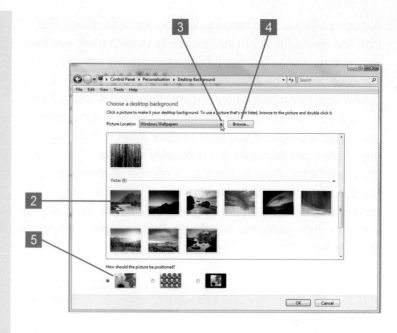

1. Click Desktop Background in the Personalisation menu.

2. To select a new background image click one of the thumbnails in the preview.

3. Choose pictures from alternative locations or select a solid colour.

4. You can select images from other folders on your hard disk by clicking the Browse button.

5. Click one of these options to choose how desktop backgrounds will be displayed. You can have it stretch the image to fill the screen, tile, or centre.

Important

Desktop backgrounds look their best when their size matches the resolution of your desktop. If they're too small, the image will be stretched or centred with a border, too large and they'll be distorted.

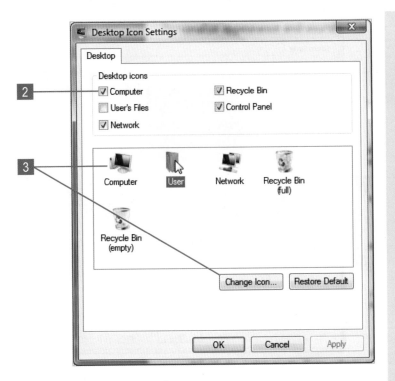

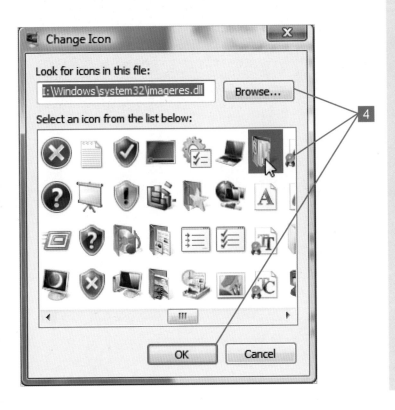

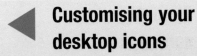
1 Click Change Desktop Icons from the Tasks list to open the Desktop Icon Settings window.

2 Click the checkboxes to remove system icons from the desktop.

3 Select an icon and click Change Icon to choose another icon graphic.

4 To apply a new icon select it from the list and click OK. You can also browse your system for other icon files.

2

Choosing a screen saver

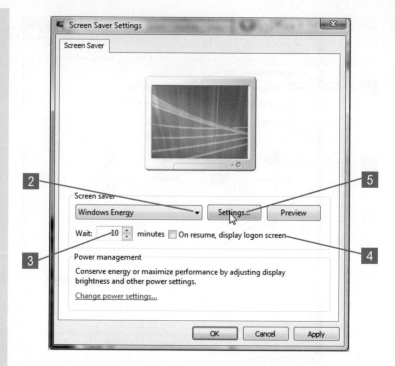

1 Click the Screen Saver option in the Personalisation menu.

2 Choose a new screen saver from the drop-down list.

3 Set a time for the delay between last activity and the screen saver enabling.

4 Enable the logon screen to password-protect your system. With this enabled you will have to enter your user account password to get back to the desktop.

5 Click the Settings button to access options for the currently selected screen saver. These change depending on the screen saver and may not always be available.

While you can completely change the look of Windows very easily using a theme, the appearance options give you a greater amount of control as you can change the colours and fonts of specific windows.

Creating your own Windows colour scheme

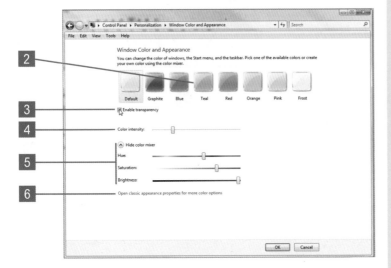

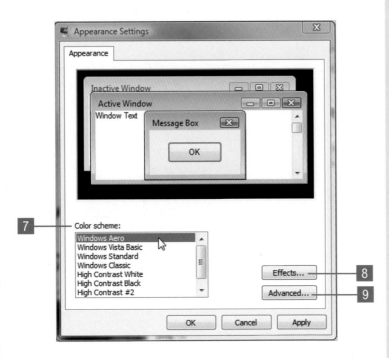

1 Open the Personalisation options and click Window Colour and Appearance.

2 Click to select one of the preset colours.

3 Transparency allows you to see the contents of windows underneath the current one.

4 Drag to increase or decrease the brightness of colours.

5 Create your own custom colours with the colour mixer by adjusting the hue, saturation and brightness sliders.

6 Click this link to access further appearance settings.

7 Select a pre-set colour scheme from the list. The preview window will change to show the new scheme.

8 Click Effects to choose Window and font effects.

9 Advanced allows you to further customise the appearance of your desktop.

Setting additional options

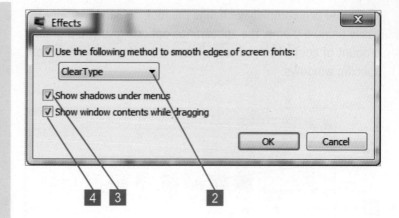

1 Click the Effects button from the Appearance settings window.

2 Font smoothing removes the jagged edges from text. ClearType font smoothing is specifically designed for flat-panel displays and it does make text appear noticeably clearer.

3 Enable or disable drop-shadows on menus.

4 By default, window contents are shown when dragging. Disable this and it will show an outline of the window instead.

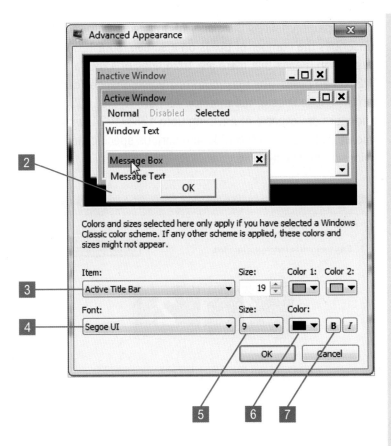

1 Back in the Appearance window click the Advanced button.

2 Use the preview window to not only see the effects of your changes, but also select which areas you want to edit by clicking them in the preview. The selected area will then appear in the Item box.

3 Use the Item box to select the part of Windows that you want to customise.

4 When applicable, the font box allows you to choose an alternative font for various window elements.

5 Use the size options to adjust the size of window elements and fonts.

6 Select a colour for the windows and text. Click Other in the colour pop-up box to create a custom colour.

7 Choose between bold and italic text styles. Click the current selection to remove all styling.

Setting a resolution and colour quality

▶

The resolution defines the clarity of an image. With monitors, it describes the number of pixels on a screen, so a 1280x1024 resolution means that there are 1024 lines of 1280, a total of 1,310,720 pixels. The maximum resolution changes depending on the capabilities of the monitor. All new 17–19" LCD monitors are capable of anything upto 1280x1024, with larger monitors handing 1600x1200 and various specifications for widescreen displays.

1 Monitor and graphics card options are found under the Display Settings link within the Personalisation menu.

2 Use the slider to change resolution. Do not take this over the maximum resolution for your monitor.

3 The colour quality should always be 32-bit. Only old systems will be incapable of handling 32-bit colour. Time to upgrade if yours can't handle it!

4 If you have multiple monitors connected to your system they'll be shown here. Click and drag these icons to match their actual location on your desk, and click them to adjust the resolution for each display. If you want to disable a monitor or set one as the primary display, right-click for further options.

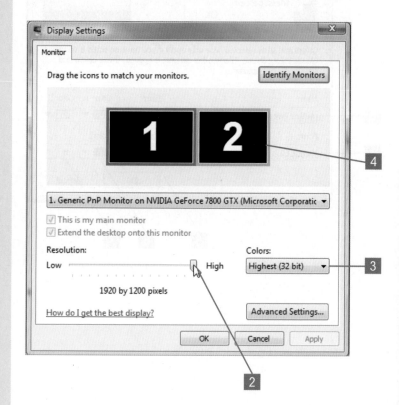

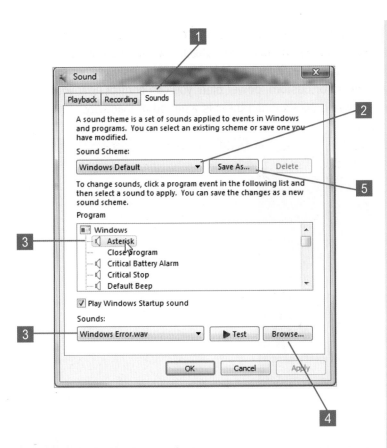

1 Go to the Personalisation menu and click Sounds.

2 Two sound schemes are included – Windows Default and No Sounds. Select one from the list and it'll ask if you want to save the previous scheme.

3 To customise the sounds, choose an event from the Program Events list and then select a sound from the list.

4 You can use any WAV audio file on your computer, just click Browse and locate the file you wish to use. Press the Play button to preview the sound.

5 Click Save As once you've configured your custom sound profile and give it a name. It'll then be added to the Sound Scheme drop-down list.

Adjusting power settings

To help conserve energy, keep your electricity bills down and extend the life of your computer there are a number of power-saving features built into Windows Vista. Using either a pre-defined or custom 'power plan' you can control how your system behaves when there is a period of inactivity.

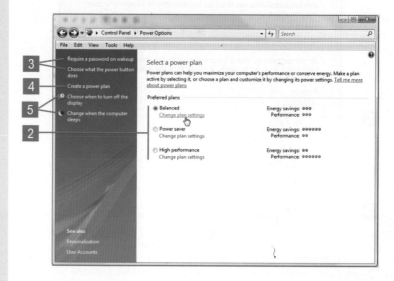

1 Power options are accessible either through the control panel or by clicking the link in the screen saver window, via the Personalisation menu.

2 Activate a power plan by clicking the radio button next to it.

3 Both of these links take you to the same dialogue box, and allow you to enable a password when coming out of sleep mode and change what happens when you press the power switch on your PC.

4 Create a new power plan using an existing plan as a template.

5 Select how long Windows will wait before switching off your monitor or entering sleep mode. This affects the currently selected power plan.

Important

For mission-critical systems an Uninterruptible Power Supply, or UPS, protects data in the event of a power failure by acting as a battery backup. Previously, a UPS would only be found on corporate servers and other important systems but simple UPS devices can now be purchased for the home user. While these do not have comparable features to a 'proper' UPS, they can act as a safety barrier when the electricity fails, giving you enough time to save your work and safely shut down the system. On desktop systems, Windows can detect a UPS device and monitor the power levels, the controls for which can be found in the Power options.

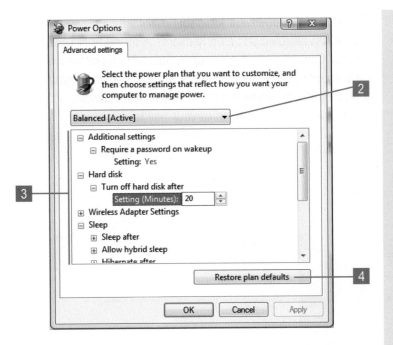

Configuring Advanced Power Settings

1 To access further power settings, click Change plan settings, then Change advanced power settings.

2 Select a power plan from the drop-down menu.

3 Scroll through the list of options and customise the plan to your needs.

4 If you make a mistake or want to start from scratch, click the Restore plan defaults button to reset the current plan to its default settings.

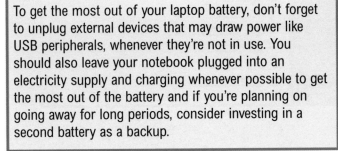

Timesaver tip

To get the most out of your laptop battery, don't forget to unplug external devices that may draw power like USB peripherals, whenever they're not in use. You should also leave your notebook plugged into an electricity supply and charging whenever possible to get the most out of the battery and if you're planning on going away for long periods, consider investing in a second battery as a backup.

Using the Ease of Acess Centre

Included in Windows are tools that make your PC easier to use and assist disabled and elderly users, all found in the Ease of Access Centre, a new feature with Vista. If you are hard of hearing, partially sighted or suffer some other disability that would otherwise make it difficult to use your computer, these settings can be customised to your needs, so you don't have to miss out. As you'll see, these are easy to use and may be helpful even if you don't have any special requirements.

1 Open the Control Panel and find the Ease of Access Centre

2 Enable these two options and Windows will read the text in the Access Centre aloud.

3 These shortcuts give you quick access to four commonly accessed features.

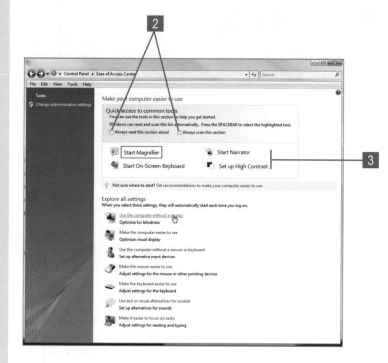

The text-to-speech capability built into Windows Vista proves extremely useful for anyone who has difficulty reading the screen. It uses a synthesised speech engine to interpret and read out on-screen text from any application or document.

Using your computer without a display

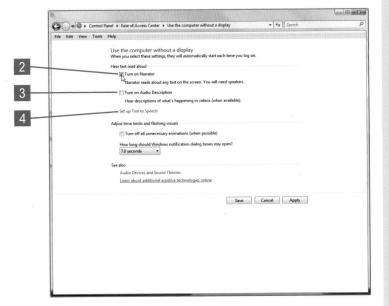

1 Click Use the computer without a display from the Ease of Access Centre.

2 Windows includes its own text-to-speech engine and when this is enabled the Narrator will read out on-screen text as you navigate.

3 Audio Descriptions will narrate videos when you watch content that has been designed to include descriptions.

4 Configure Windows' text-to-speech features. You can choose from several voices and adjust the speed.

Adjusting the display settings

Further assistance for users with impaired vision can be found within the Access Centre. There is a high contrast graphics mode that makes text more visible and the magnifier option shows a zoomed-in display wherever the mouse is pointing.

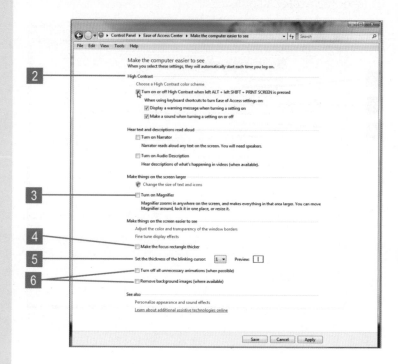

1 Click Make the computer easier to see in the Access Centre.

2 These High Contrast settings come into effect when you select a high contrast scheme from the appearance menu. To change schemes, click the link or go to the Personalise menu.

3 The magnifier zooms the view to make it easier to see your desktop. You can also click the link above to increase or decrease the font size.

4 Making the focus rectangle thicker means it's easier to see which window is currently selected.

5 Increase the thickness of the blinking mouse cursor.

6 Remove images and animations that may be unnecessary or distracting.

One important new feature in Windows Vista is the speech recognition that translates your speech to text. All you need is a microphone connected to your computer. The speech recognition feature can be accessed either through the Control Panel or the Access Centre.

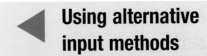
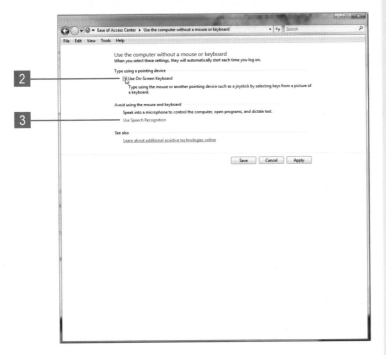

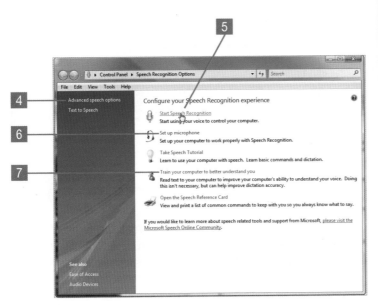

1 Click Use the computer without a mouse or keyboard in the Access Centre.

2 The on-screen keyboard allows you to use a pointing device to input text, and is useful for tablet PCs with touch-sensitive displays.

3 Click this link to configure speech recognition.

4 Access more speech recognition options here, including a setting that loads speech recognition each time Windows loads.

5 Manually start speech recognition. If you've not configured speech recognition previously it will ask you to do so before continuing.

6 Configure your microphone to enable speech recognition.

7 By default, the speech recognition software will be able to understand you, but if you use the training function you can greatly increase the number of words it recognises and correctly transcribes.

Adjusting mouse settings

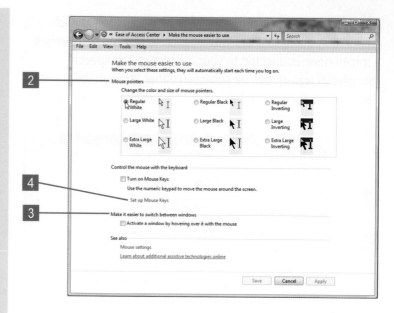

1. In the Access Centre click Make the mouse easier to use.

2. You can select several different mouse pointer settings to make them easier to see.

3. Enabling this option will select windows when you hover over them with the mouse cursor, instead of clicking.

4. Enabling mouse keys will let you move the cursor using the directional keys on the numerical keypad. Click Set Up Mouse Keys to configure this feature.

5. Click here to run Mouse Keys with a keyboard shortcut. Unfortunately you cannot select the shortcut keys yourself.

6. These options will come into play each time you enable an accessibility feature with a shortcut.

7. Use these sliders to adjust the top speed and acceleration of the mouse pointer when controlling it with Mouse Keys.

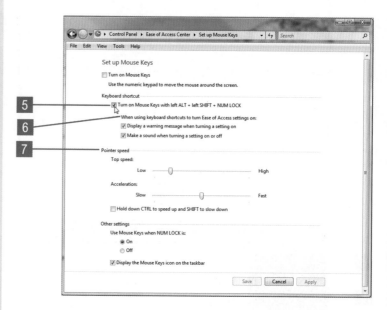

Timesaver tip

If the text on a website is too small to read, hold down Ctrl and spin the mouse wheel to zoom in and out. This also works in some other applications, such as word processors.

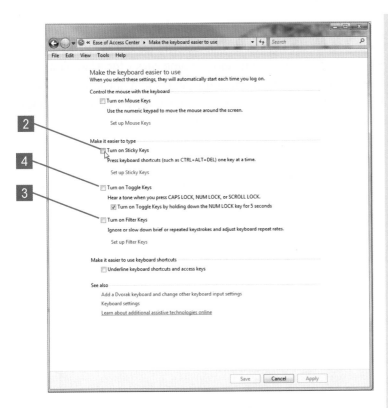

Adjusting keyboard settings

1 In the Ease of Access Centre, click the keyboard option.

2 Sticky Keys makes Ctrl, Alt, Shift and the Windows key behave like Caps Lock – you will only need to press these once to use them and once more to turn them off.

3 Filter Keys will stop a key being repeated if it's held down or it can ignore repeated keystrokes.

4 With Toggle Keys enabled you will hear a noise when Caps Lock, Num Lock and Scroll Lock are pressed.

Changing the keyboard language

During the installation of Windows Vista you'll set the language options for the keyboard. This determines the keyboard layout and will change the function of some keys - for example the pound sign on a UK keyboard changes to a dollar sign if you set it to US layout. If you need to change the keyboard settings later you can easily do so via the Control Panel.

1 Open the Control Panel and click Regional and Language Options.

2 Click the Keyboards and Languages tab.

3 In the General tab you can select a new language by clicking the Add button, or choose one of the installed languages from the drop-down menu.

4 The Language Bar allows you to quickly swap between multiple languages. It is enabled by default and can either be docked on the taskbar or free-floating on the desktop.

5 In Advanced Key Settings you can enable a keyboard shortcut for swapping languages. The keys used for this can be customised here.

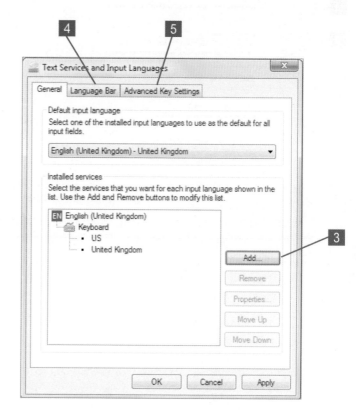

3 [3]

Enabling audio and visual helpers

1 Click Use text or visual alternatives for sounds.

2 Sound Sentry will visibly alert you when the system makes a sound. You can choose the method it uses from the drop-down menu.

3 Enabling this feature will display captions for spoken dialogue whenever it is available.

2

3

Security and privacy

Introduction

Security is a big buzzword in modern computing. Keeping the contents of your hard drive safe from the prying eyes of others is an uphill battle, and with the advent of broadband meaning more and more users are logging on every day, the risk of exposing your files and folders to the masses has increased exponentially over the last few years. Luckily, the 'good guys', security software vendors and Microsoft themselves have been working round the clock to stay ahead of the hackers, data-collectors and spies. Improvements to the Windows operating system, and a wide range of free or very reasonably priced security software, has actually made it easier than ever before to protect your machine. One of the biggest innovations of recent times has actually been made possible due to the success of broadband. Live updates are now common across not only antivirus software but firewalls and anti ad-ware and spy-ware tools, meaning that definitions to defeat the latest security loopholes and viruses can be made available to you seconds after they are conceived. In this chapter we'll show you how to beef up security on your home PC, and we're focusing on ease of use as well, so even the least ambitious of beginners will have no trouble setting up a shield to beat away the malicious masses.

Jargon buster

Broadband – traditionally the name given to a service which uses a single wire to carry many signals, for example, cable telephone services that also provide television. Recently it has been applied to fast Internet connections, though ISPs will call anything from 256k upwards broadband when many don't believe that is true broadband and it's not fast enough. Most broadband connections now are at least 512k.

What you'll do

Secure Windows

Configure Windows Update

Control services and processes

Use Windows Security Centre

Configure the Windows Firewall

Control user access

Change parental controls

Protect your system from viruses

Use and configure AVG Anti-Virus

Use Windows Firewall

Protect your system from spyware using Spybot

Protect your system with passwords and encryption

Lock and encrypt files and folders

Understand wireless network security

Securing Windows

Before we even get onto installing firewalls and antivirus applications, there are a number of steps you should take to secure Windows. Microsoft provides an auto-update service and it's absolutely vital that you use this regularly to keep your system protected. Security holes are discovered frequently and the Windows Update service will help safeguard your system by installing the security fixes. It's also a smart idea to learn how to monitor your system for changes. There are plenty of programs – both malicious and benign – that will attempt to place themselves in the System Tray or load with Windows, so keeping an eye on what's going on in the background can help you minimise security risks as well as system clutter.

Patch your system with Windows Update

1 Open the Control Panel and click Windows Update.

2 Click Check for updates to get the latest update information from Microsoft.

3 The optional updates will vary depending on the version of Windows Vista you are using. Windows Vista Ultimate owners get free extra software.

4 The file size and time to download of selected updates is shown here. Important updates are automatically selected, click Install to begin downloading those, while others must be chosen by clicking View available updates.

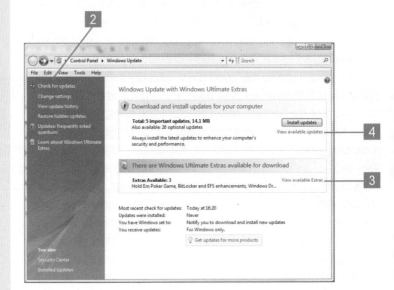

Jargon buster

Virus – software program created for the purpose of causing damage to the system it infects. Some viruses simply damage files, others take over the systems and allow them to be remotely controlled, turning them into 'zombies'. This can be dangerous, as there have been cases where zombie systems are used to store pornography and pirated software without the knowledge of the owner.

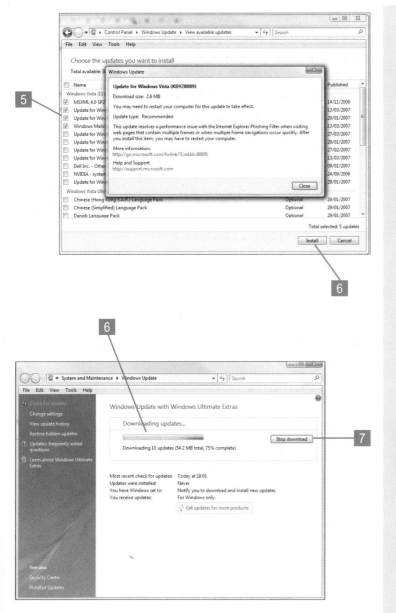

5 To add an update to the download list click the box next to its entry, click the box at the top of the column to add every update. Right-click and choose View Details to see a description of the update.

6 Select all the updates you want, then click install. (Download time will vary depending on the size and number of updates and the speed of your connection.)

7 Halt the update process if you need to.

8 After the updates have been downloaded you will be prompted to restart your computer. You should always do this before you continue using it.

3

Configuring Windows Update

Windows Update includes options for unassisted updates, with three levels of automation available. It can either download and install new updates at a specific time each day without asking you; download updates but ask if you want to install them; or just check for new updates and prompt you to choose which should be downloaded and installed. We highly recommend that you enable the automatic option as it means you'll always be protected with the latest patches.

1 In Windows Update click Change settings. This section contains options for configuring Automatic Updates and notifications.

2 Choose either full automation, download updates automatically or check for updates only. If you choose full automatic updates you'll need to choose a time and date.

3 You can also disable updates completely, but unless there's a very good reason, you should never do this.

4 Check this option to include recommended updates in the update process. Recommended updates are less critical patches that fix bugs and add new features, but which are not dealing with any immediate security threat.

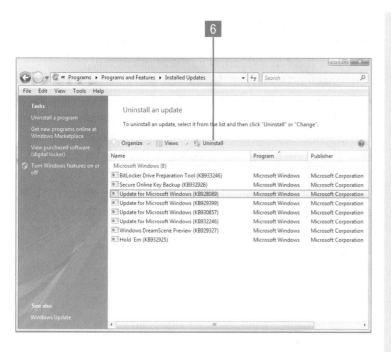

Configuring Windows Update (cont.)

5 If you find an update causes problems you can remove it by clicking Installed Updates from within Windows Update. You can also view previously installed or aborted updates with View Update History.

6 Installed Updates is part of the Programs and Features tool and works the same way as removing an application. Select the update you wish to remove from the list then press Uninstall.

3

Controlling services and background processes

Open the Configuration Tool

1 Click the Start menu and choose the Run command. If Run is not available, you'll need to enable it by opening Start menu properties, clicking Customise and then enabling the Run command in the list of options.

2 Type 'Msconfig' into the text box that appears and press Return to load the Microsoft Configuration Tool.

Whenever Windows starts up, it initialises a number of processes in order to get itself ready for your use. These are programs that run invisibly in the background, and offer additional functionality or provide you with access to additional tools or accessibility features. Processes are often employed and started by applications you've installed to your hard drive, such as virus-checkers that keep running in the background to keep your system free from infection. If you've installed a lot of software for various reasons since you've had your machine, you might find you have an inordinate amount of these services and processes running, many of which may not actually be necessary for the day-to-day running of your computer. It must be stressed at this point that stopping services or processes that are vital to the running of Windows or its installed applications may cause problems and you may find programs cease to run. It's fairly easy to revert back to your original settings but you should take care when carrying out these sorts of changes to your operating system regardless. Successfully removing services or processes that aren't needed can not only improve the overall security of your system but speed up your machine as well. All of this can be accomplished by using the built-in Microsoft Configuration Tool.

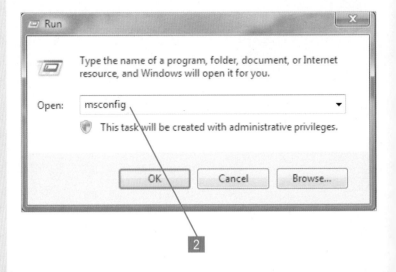

The Startup options give you three choices for booting your system. By default, the Selective Startup is used, which uses system files set up with specific processes and services to load. You can choose to run a full boot, which loads everything on your system or the Diagnostic Startup to load basic drivers only. If you have problems starting your system or running applications after making changes, you can try booting with one of these alternative options.

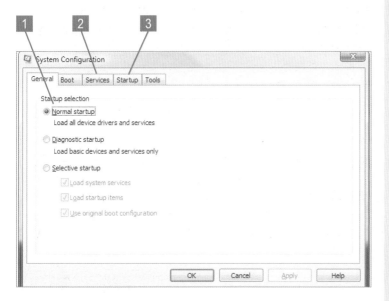

1 Select an appropriate startup option, if required.

2 The Services tab is one way to change the services that load with Windows or to stop services that are currently running. An alternative method here is to use the Component Services tool, which we'll look at a bit later.

3

3 The Startup tab shows the software that loads when your computer boots up, much of which may well be unnecessary. A bit later, we'll show you how to prevent software or add-ons you don't really need from booting with Windows.

Using MSConfig (cont.)

Use the MSConfig Startup tab

1 The left column in this list is the name of the Startup Item running on your computer. The name may not always make it obvious exactly what process this item is starting, so you'll need to use the other two columns here to help.

2 The third column shows the command line of the process that is running. This is the command 'executable' and any associated parameters used to start the process. The path in this string should give you a good idea of exactly which application is utilising this process.

3 These two buttons are simply shortcuts to enabling or disabling all of the processes at once, and isn't usually recommended. You should pick and choose processes to stop or restart based on what you know from the filename and path of the process. Use the tickboxes alongside individual rows to control particular processes.

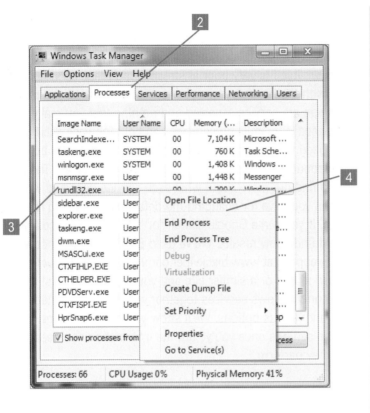

1 Task Manager used to be accessed directly by pressing Ctrl+Alt+Del, but this has changed slightly – now you press Ctrl+Alt+Del and click Start Task Manager from the list of options.

2 Click the Processes tab to view the processes currently running on your computer.

3 Right-click a process to raise its priority with your operating system or, more commonly, to terminate it if you suspect it is causing problems with your machine.

4 Click Open File Location to go to the folder where the selected program is stored.

3

Editing and configuring Windows Services

Windows uses a myriad of services to control the day-to-day running of your PC and prepare itself for the various tasks you might want to complete during a session. For the most part, Windows itself is very poor at streamlining these services to cope with the tasks you use your computer for, and you may find there are services enabled and running that you really don't need. Streamlining services can both increase security and speed up your machine, so it's worth reading up a bit more about them in case you want to do this yourself. The best way to find out more about what each service does and what options you have for changing the default settings is to read up online. If you run a Google search for 'Windows Services' you should find a few results. We've used Black Viper's Windows Vista webpage at www.blackviper.com/WinVista/servicecfg.htm. Browse to this or a similar site and you should see a list of common Windows services together with better explanations and your various options. We'll show you how to change your service settings once you've got the information you need on how they perform.

1 The Black Viper homepage provides you with plenty of information on Windows services, and will tell you what settings to use for services depending on how you want to use your PC.

2 As a summary guide, the corresponding table shows the service settings for different categories of computer. Once you've familiarised yourself with each category you can scan through this table to check the service setting and change your services as you see fit.

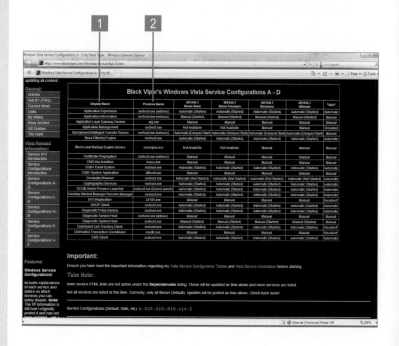

62

Important

Stopping processes, and particularly changing service settings, are Windows tweaks that can cause problems if you're not sure what you're doing. If you do decide you want to streamline your machine by shutting down processes you deem unnecessary, it's not advisable to make widespread changes in one go. Instead of turning off eight processes and disabling twenty services in one go, for example, do two or three at a time and then reboot your machine. If you can perform all the usual operations and open applications without problems, change a few more and reboot again. This way if something does go wrong it'll be far easier to work out exactly what may be causing the problem.

3

Accessing the Administrative Tools

The Computer Management utility is a set of tools for modifying the configuration of your PC. You need to be logged in as an Administrator to modify these settings.

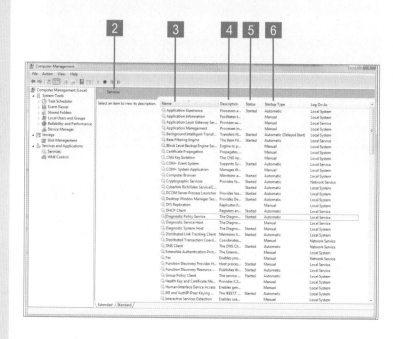

1 Open the Control Panel and double-click Administrative Tools, then double click Computer Management.

2 Click Services and Applications then Services.

3 The first column shows the name of the process, which may be referred to in error messages, instructions or guides to manipulating your Windows environment as you delve deeper into modifying the setup of your PC.

4 The description column should give you some idea of exactly what the service does and perhaps how vital it is to the way you run your machine.

5 The status column informs you whether or not the process is currently started and running on your system.

6 The startup type column tells you how Windows treats the service on bootup. Some services are started automatically, others need to be manually started and others may be disabled altogether.

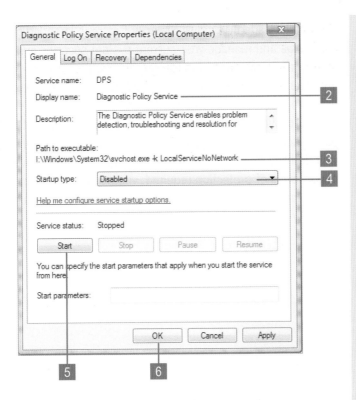

Diagnostic Policy Service Properties (Local Computer)

General | Log On | Recovery | Dependencies

Service name: DPS

Display name: Diagnostic Policy Service — **2**

Description: The Diagnostic Policy Service enables problem detection, troubleshooting and resolution for

Path to executable:
I:\Windows\System32\svchost.exe -k LocalServiceNoNetwork — **3**

Startup type: Disabled — **4**

Help me configure service startup options.

Service status: Stopped

[Start] [Stop] [Pause] [Resume]

You can specify the start parameters that apply when you start the service from here.

Start parameters:

[OK] [Cancel] [Apply]

5   **6**

Changing Service settings

1 To change Service settings, right-click the service and choose Properties from the context menu.

2 You'll find the name of the service and a description of how it affects your machine at the top of this window.

3 The path to the executable file that runs the service, along with any parameters that are included is shown here.

4 The Startup Type can be changed from this dropdown list. You can choose whether to automatically or manually start the service, or disable it altogether.

5 If you change the settings, they may not take effect until you restart your computer. To start, stop, pause or resume a service without restarting your computer use the command buttons shown here.

6 Click the OK or Apply button to enforce any changes you've made, or the Cancel button to disregard them and revert to the service's original state.

3

Using Windows Security Centre

The much needed Windows Security Centre is intended to help you gauge and manage your current system security, and makes far more sense than trawling through a series of unrelated menus and windows to find the firewall settings, for example. Open the Security Centre and you'll find it not only relates to Microsoft's built-in security, but keeps track of third party security software you have installed on your system as well. Initially reassuring as a brief summary that you have the major levels of protection required, you can also find out more about each type of security and tweak and adjust the built-in Windows tools like the Windows Firewall.

1 The firewall settings let you know if either the Windows Firewall or a third party firewall is currently enabled on your operating system.

2 The automatic updates setting is important in order to receive the latest security updates and Windows enhancements.

3 Virus protection is essential for any modern PC. If you have third-party antivirus software installed it will register here.

4 Windows Defender is Microsoft's own anti-spyware tool. You may wish to continue using your own anti-spyware application, but Defender is free so it's definitely worth leaving it enabled.

5 Click the arrows next to any of the items to read more about the importance of this type of security.

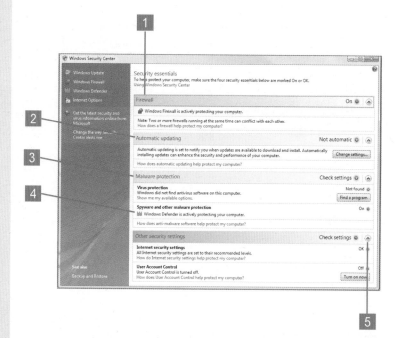

Jargon buster

Firewall – a barrier between the Internet and your computer. It protects from outside threats like viruses and hackers by filtering the incoming data, blocking any potentially harmful information. Firewalls are an absolute vital part of any system connected to the Internet.

Despite the addition of a more user-friendly Security Centre, the firewall is no easier to use, and only advanced users will be comfortable adjusting the settings using the tools on offer. We'll show you how to install a more useful, friendly and far more configurable firewall a bit later in this chapter.

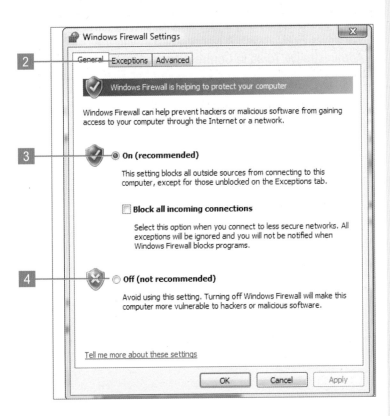

1 Open the Firewall by clicking Windows Firewall in Security Centre, then click Change Settings.

2 You can use the tabbed list along the top to view the current settings, open ports or add exceptions to your current firewall configuration.

3 Click the On button to turn the firewall on if you don't already have one installed. If you're currently working without any firewall, you should turn on the Windows Firewall now, at least for the time being,

4 If you have another firewall installed you can leave the Windows Firewall off by choosing the Off option.

For your information

If you use a wireless router to connect to the Internet it will very likely include a firewall built-in. The firewalls on routers are powerful and unobtrusive, so if you haven't already you should enable it to protect yourself even further. The Windows Firewall is still useful, however, as it allows you to control Internet access for specific applications.

Configuring Windows Firewall (cont.)

Timesaver tip

The Windows Firewall includes some more advanced settings that can give an even greater level of control over your connection. These are slightly harder to find but if you fancy having a play around you can find the Windows Firewall with Advanced Security in the Administrative Tools in Control Panel.

The ability to handle multiple users as standard was introduced with Windows XP to give families and those working from home or on shared machines a chance to have their own individual settings and access privileges. From a convenience point of view it's a great way to avoid arguments and keep your own personalised desktops and folder structure, but it also has a strong security benefit if you work on a shared machine. By setting up and using multiple accounts you can install different applications for each user and restrict access to critical parts of the operating system. Files and folders that you've created will only be visible to you, so when you log off you can be sure that the next user won't be able to access the files you've just created.

Whether or not you consider a shared machine to be a security risk, it's worth setting up user accounts so you can control user access anyway, and is very easy to do.

 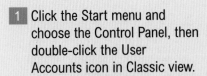

Controlling user access

1. Click the Start menu and choose the Control Panel, then double-click the User Accounts icon in Classic view.

2. Add a password to your account. When a password is present this disappears and is replaced by Change Password and Remove Password options.

3. Change the picture associated with your account.

4. Change the name of your account.

5. Select a different account type, with fewer or more access privileges depending on your current account level.

6. Change the settings for another account.

7. Disable or enable User Account Control.

3

Jargon buster

User switching – a Windows option that allows you to quickly switch from one user account to another without losing data.

Controlling user access (cont.)

Jargon buster

UAC – User Account Control. A new security feature in Windows Vista that asks the user to enter a password to authorise an application.

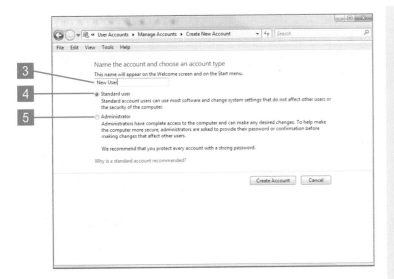

Name the account and choose an account type

This name will appear on the Welcome screen and on the Start menu.

New User

⦿ Standard user
Standard account users can use most software and change system settings that do not affect other users or the security of the computer.

◯ Administrator
Administrators have complete access to the computer and can make any desired changes. To help make the computer more secure, administrators are asked to provide their password or confirmation before making changes that affect other users.

We recommend that you protect every account with a strong password.

Why is a standard account recommended?

Create Account   Cancel

Creating a new user account

1 Click Manage another account from the User Accounts window.

2 Select Create a new account

3 Enter a name for the account.

4 If you choose a standard user account, the new user will be able to make changes to their account and files and adjust non-critical system settings.

5 Administrator gives a user total control over the system. For the best security you should only have one Administrator account that is used when you need to install some application or make changes to the settings, otherwise every user should log in with a standard acccount.

3

For your information

User Account Control (UAC) is a new security feature that aims to protect your PC from damaging programs. When an application tries to access certain areas of your system, you're given a prompt asking you to enter the username and password of an Administrator to continue running the software or, if you are using an Administrator account, to allow or deny access. While it has good intentions many find this feature very irritating as it will often appear to be asking you to authorise legitimate applications. So long as you exercise the usual caution and do not run software without scanning it for viruses, it's perfectly safe to disable UAC, though it does prove useful for restricting access to your computer for children or other users sharing the PC.

Jargon buster

Shared folder – one that's accessible to other users of the same computer or network.

Running as Administrator

When enabled, User Access Control should automatically pop up and prompt you to enter the administrator password in order to allow an application to continue. If it doesn't, you may need to manually run an application as Administrator.

1 Locate the executable file for an application. This can either be its shortcut on the desktop or Start Menu, or the .exe file itself, located in the program directory.

2 Right-click on a file and choose 'Run as administrator'. Enter your administrator password into the window that appears and the program will load.

Jargon buster

Computer Administrator – when applied to user accounts, an Administrator is a person who has full access to the entire system, including the ability to install and remove software and other administration tasks. When applied to networks and corporate systems, the Administrator is the person in charge of maintaining the systems.

Timesaver tip

The administrator password is like the key to your house – you don't just give it out to anybody. When sharing a system you should limit administrator access to one account and use that only to control the system. Standard users are still able to run applications and make changes to their personal settings, like desktop wallpapers and so on, but they are not allowed to modify anything that will affect the system. For security you should use standard accounts on a day-to-day basis, only utilising the administrator password when necessary.

Experienced Windows XP users will be aware that an Administrator account is configured when the operating system is installed, but hidden from view by default for security. This is also true of Windows Vista, and you can easily enable this Administrator account so it appears on the main login screen. This is convenient but keep the password from anybody you don't want having total access to the computer.

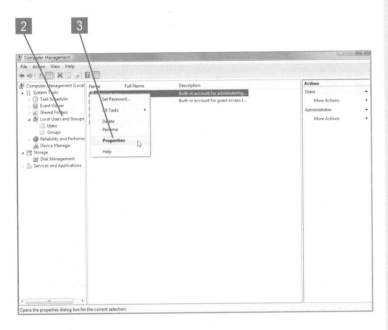

Enabling the default Administrator account

1 First ensure you're logged into an account with Administrator rights, then right-click on Computer (from the desktop or Start Menu) and click Manage.

2 Expand the Local Users and Groups option and click Users.

3 Right-click on Administrator and click Properties.

3

Timesaver tip

The options found in Computer Management provide additional, in-depth controls for users on your system. The same setting used to enable the Administrator account in the task above can also be used to make other accounts inaccessible, and also within that same Properties window are several options for controlling the user passwords. By default a password will never expire, but for extra security you can switch this off and force the user to select a new password after 42 days. You could also stop them from ever changing the password, or enable both the password expiry and disable the password changing, so that the user will be unable to access their account after the time has run out.

Enabling the default Administrator account (cont.)

4 In the General tab remove the check from the 'Account is disabled' option.

5 Close the Properties window and then Computer Management. Now whenever you go to the Windows Vista login you'll find an Administrator account alongside the other users.

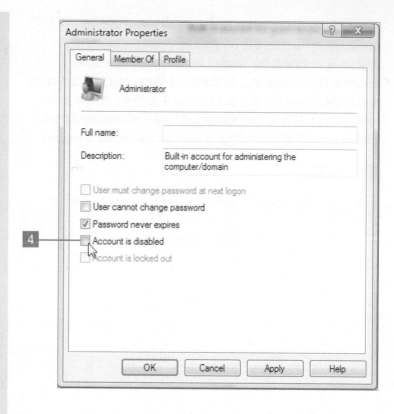

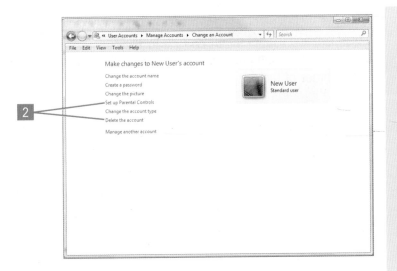

Editing user accounts

1. After a new account is created you'll be back in the Manage Accounts window. Click an account to change its settings.

2. These options are essentially identical to those found in your own account controls, with additional delete and parental control settings.

3. When you click Delete you have the option of keeping the user's deleted files. These will be placed on your desktop in a folder named after their account.

3

Changing parental controls

Windows Vista's parental controls let you specify exactly what a user can and cannot do on your PC by blocking or allowing certain websites and programs or even only allowing access at certain times of the day.

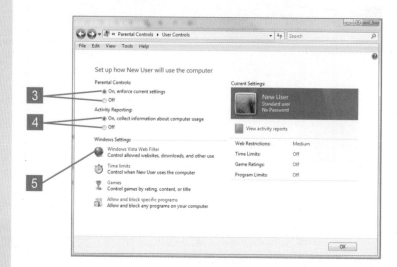

1. Click a user account in Manage Accounts, then click Set up parental controls.

2. Choose the account for which you want to set up parental controls. You must be using an Administrator account with a password to do this. If the Administrator account has no password any user may change the parental control settings.

3. Enable parental controls.

4. Enable or disable activity reporting, which records websites visited, downloads, applications and more.

5. Click the web filter option to limit Internet access.

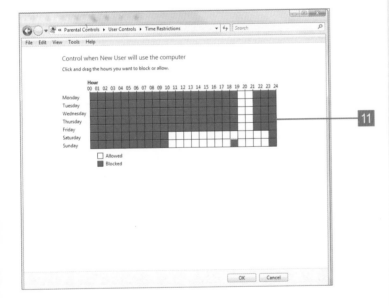

Changing parental controls (cont.)

6 Using web filters you can either allow all sites – disabling the rest of the web filter options – or customise the filter list to block or only allow access to certain pages.

7 Click Edit the Allow and block list to specify websites which are to be filtered. If you check the Only allow ... option the user will not see any sites except those you enter in the list.

8 The automatic filters will attempt to block access without user input to certain types of websites. You can choose three varying levels for the filter or customise its settings.

9 Check this option to stop the user from downloading files.

10 In the parental controls, click Time limits.

11 The time limit controls are very simple: just click or drag the mouse to fill in the blocks of time in blue and the user will not be able to use the PC during those periods. To remove a block, just click once on a blue square to turn it white.

Changing parental controls (cont.)

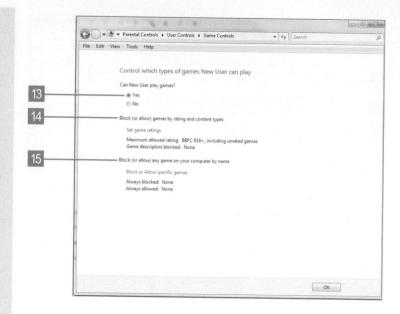

12 To control the type of games a user can play, or block them entirely, go to Parental Controls and click Games.

13 If you wish, you can stop a user from playing any games.

14 One useful option if you have young children is to deny access to games based on their age rating. Click here to define the maximum rating.

15 Block a specific game by name.

16 To stop users running a program, click Allow and block specific programs in Parental Controls.

17 To restrict who has access to certain programs, click New User can only use the programs I allow.

18 Windows will search and list all the programs it can find on your hard drive.

19 If a program is missing click Browse to add it to the list.

20 Check the boxes next to each program you wish to let the user access.

21 If you enable activity reporting you can see what the user has been getting up to by choosing View activity reports in the Parental Controls.

22 The summary will show the most recent activity, including data on games, email and instant messaging.

23 Expand the categories in the tree to see more detailed reports for specific types of activity.

3

Creating a password reset disk

Securing user accounts with a password protects the files within each user directory, so you can safely store your documents, email and programs out of sight of other users on the system, and prevents unauthorised access to your system. If you happen to forget your administrator password, though, you are locked out of the system, so to prevent this from happening it's a smart idea to create a password reset disk with which you can regain control of your Administrator account if the password slips your mind. Obviously this can be used for evil as well as good, so make sure to keep it somewhere safe. It's important to note that this process needs to be done before you forget the password, not after!

1 Go to User Accounts in the Control Panel. Click Create a password reset disk in the Tasks list.

2 Read the information presented in the dialogue box and click Next.

3 Select the drive containing the disk you wish to use. This can be a floppy disk, but as floppy drives are increasingly rare in new systems you may not have that option. Instead, use a USB flash drive.

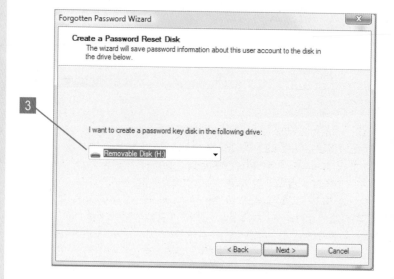

Forgotten Password Wizard

Create a Password Reset Disk
The wizard will save password information about this user account to the disk in the drive below.

3

I want to create a password key disk in the following drive:

Removable Disk (H:)

< Back   Next >   Cancel

Timesaver tip

Using the reset disk is easy. Start your PC as normal – don't insert the disk yet – and when you get to the login screen try to enter a password for the account. If it doesn't work, insert the recovery disk, wait a second, then use the reset option. Just follow the wizard that appears to choose a new password.

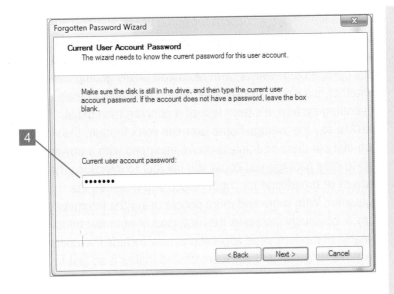

Forgotten Password Wizard

Current User Account Password
The wizard needs to know the current password for this user account.

Make sure the disk is still in the drive, and then type the current user account password. If the account does not have a password, leave the box blank.

Current user account password:

•••••••

< Back   Next >   Cancel

4

4 Enter the password for your Administrator account, click Next, and wait for the process to complete.

3

For your information

USB flash drives (also called memory sticks, key drives and USB drives as well as various other names) are small devices that utilise memory chips for storing data, as opposed to the optical storage of a CD or DVD or the magnetic platters used in hard drives and floppy disks. They are usually about the size of a disposable lighter and have a USB connection on one end. When you plug them into your computer they appear as a storage device, and have essentially replaced floppy disks as a way of quickly and easily moving files. Memory sticks are cheap (less than £10 for 1GB), and more durable and flexible than a CD so it's a good idea to keep a couple handy for when you need to transport some files between different systems.

Protecting your system from viruses

Viruses are always a concern for home users, and over the last 5 years or so we've been plagued by even more infectious strains that find new and more inventive ways of making it onto our home PCs. However, with Microsoft finally getting their act together and improving security through updates to their operating system, it's been less of a concern than usual. This isn't to say the average home user can relax though, the viruses are still out there and unless you're equipped with a powerful up-to-date package you could still fall foul to infection. The advent of broadband has both helped and hindered the situation. With more and more people using the internet every day, it obviously increases the likelihood of potential infection. Nearly all modern virus applications now include live update features however, and since broadband makes it so fast to download the latest updates to upgrade your software, these strains are finding it harder to make an impact. Installing and keeping a good virus-checker up-to-date is an essential but fairly straightforward process, and something every PC user should be doing. There are a number of virus-checkers around, varying from those that are free to use to 30-day trials and retail-only versions that you have to pay subscriptions for. We're going to use the virus-checker from AVG since it's free to use and offers free updates to their online virus database. Over the next few pages we'll show you how to download and update the AVG antivirus software to keep your PC safe from harm.

1. Browse to the free AVG download site at http://free.grisoft.com. Click the AVG Anti-Virus Free link on the left.

2. Read the information about the AVG Anti-Virus. Take note of the section detailing what you don't receive in the free edition - if any of that sounds important you should consider paying for the full version.

3. Click the download link to get your own copy of AVG Anti-Virus Free.

Jargon buster

Live updates – allow a program to download new versions of itself or, in the case of spyware and antivirus tools, new information about threats to keep your system protected. Generally, live updates should be done in the background without requiring any user intervention.

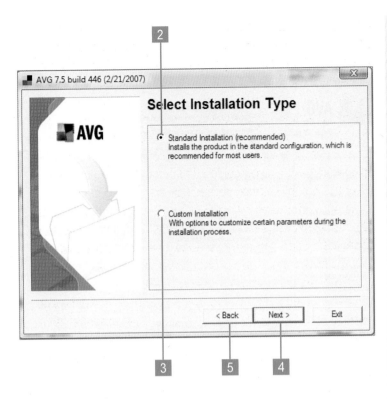

Choose an installation type

1 Once the software has finished downloading, double-click the icon in the download location.

2 A wizard guides you through the install process. You can choose to install the standard version of the software, which is recommended for new users and includes the most commonly used settings.

3 If you know what you're doing, and want further control over configuring which parts of the software are installed, you can choose the Custom Installation, which offers you option boxes to select or deselect certain elements of the software.

4 The wizard includes Back and Next buttons to move back and forth through the installation process. Click Next to proceed after each step.

5 At any stage click Back to move back and review your selections.

Important

Antivirus websites like the Grisoft site update their news regularly to report new strains of viruses and any current virus alerts that their users should be aware of. It's worth checking back every now and again to find out if any recent viruses have appeared that you need to be aware of so you can update your software.

Protecting your system from viruses (cont.)

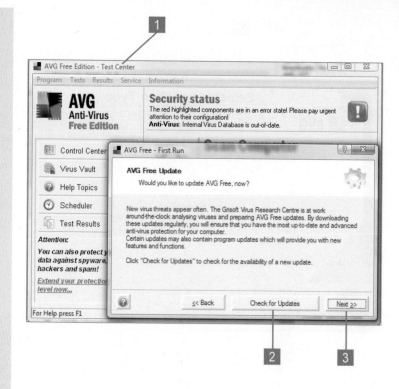

Complete the installation

1 Once installed the software will be run and you'll see the main interface appear. It is from here that you control the virus software and run scans and updates to your system.

2 The startup wizard appears the first time you run the software and allows you to perform a live update immediately to update the software with the latest virus definitions. You should do this straight away to make sure your system is protected against the latest security risks.

3 Again, the Back/Next wizard layout guides you through the initial setup procedure and gets the software ready to run on your system.

Important

Run live updates at regular intervals to keep your system as well protected as possible. Really these should be run every time Windows starts but if you don't connect to the Internet that often they can be run intermittently to keep things in check.

 From the main interface, open the Test Centre.

2 Click the Virus Vault option to see results of recent scans. You can view information on the viruses that have been detected on your system, the time and date on which they were caught, as well as which files they infected.

3 Click Help Topics for additional help with the software.

4 The Scheduler allows you to set virus scans for certain times and help you keep your system more secure by running checks at regular intervals.

5 Test Results shows all the results of recent scans – useful for keeping a track of how often your computer is being attacked and exactly what the software is protecting you from.

Configuring AVG Anti-Virus

The Control Centre options allow you to tailor the software for your system and decide what options you want it to use when scanning for viruses.

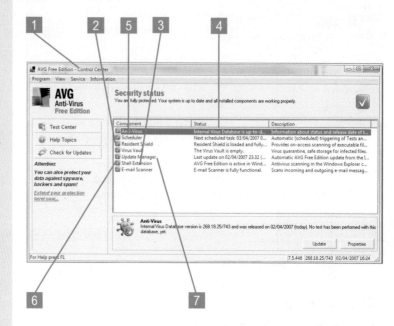

1. Open the Control Centre.

2. The AVG Resident Shield lets you choose which drives and files, and which areas of your system you want to scan.

3. The Email Scanner scans incoming and outgoing mail messages. Use its options to choose which emails to scan and how to treat them if a virus is found.

4. The Internal Virus Database stores all of the new virus definitions you can download with Live Update. It will let you know if you need to run this to keep your software up-to-date.

5. The Scheduler allows you to configure virus scans to run at certain times, or at regular intervals over the course of the week or month.

6. The Shell Extension option integrates an AVG scanning option into the right-click menu on Windows Explorer.

7. You can configure the Update Manager to run when Windows starts or whenever updates are required.

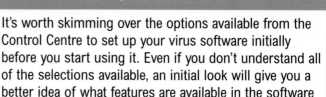

For your information

It's worth skimming over the options available from the Control Centre to set up your virus software initially before you start using it. Even if you don't understand all of the selections available, an initial look will give you a better idea of what features are available in the software and where you can go to change how AVG behaves.

1

AVG Free Edition - Test Center

Program   Tests   Results   Service   Information

AVG
Anti-Virus
Free Edition

- Control Center
- Virus Vault
- Help Topics
- Scheduler
- Test Results

Attention:
You can also protect your data against spyware, hackers and spam!
Extend your protection level now...

Security status
You are fully protected. Your system is up to date and all installed components are working properly.

Scheduled Tasks

Name	Type	Last start	Next start	Status	Scheduled for
Test plan in basic mode	Test	not started yet	03/04/2007 08:00		Current user only
Update plan in Basic mode	Update	not started yet	03/04/2007 between 08:00 and 09:59 (09:30)		Current user only

New Schedule   Edit Schedule   Delete   Close

For Help press F1   7.5.446 268.18.25/743 02/04/2007 16:24

2   **3**   **4**

Timesaver tip

Modern PCs are powerful enough to run virus scans with very little speed overheads on your system. If you have broadband and regularly use the Internet, live updates can also be performed very quickly and are relatively hassle free. For this reason it's advisable to set scans and updates to run whenever you start Windows. They are the safest bet in the long run.

Scheduling a virus scan

1 The Scheduler helps you set up automated virus scanning by choosing a time or date, or a regular interval on which to run the software and check your system. Schedules that you've configured appear in this list as a quick reference, along with the type and starting date of the next scan.

2 To create a new schedule, click this button and fill in the details as prompted. A scan will now run at the next configured interval.

3 To edit a current schedule, select one from the main list and click the Edit Schedule button. Depending on the type of test, you'll have different options available to change the date, time or interval of the scan, update or test.

4 To remove schedules select one from the list and click the delete button. Any scans you've set up on this schedule will no longer be run. If you have no scheduled scans in the list, you'll have to run all scans manually.

3

Viewing scan reports and changing test configuration

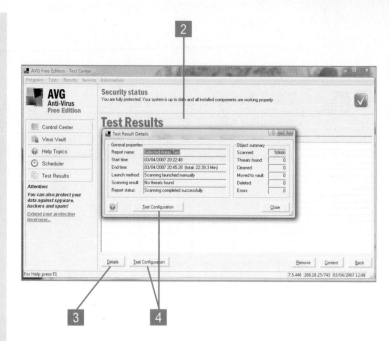

1. The Test Results button will allow you to review the results of all scans on your system, including files in which infections were found. You can also change the testing configuration from here.

2. A list of tests that have already been run appear here, at which point you can select an item from the list and use the control buttons at the bottom of the window to view more information.

3. The Details button brings up all the test details from the scan, including when it was performed and a summary of results and objects searched.

4. Change the test configuration here and choose which drives, and which parts of each individual drives are tested when a scan is run.

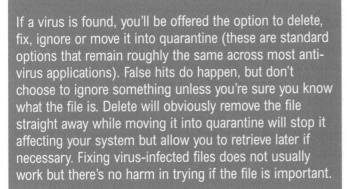

Scanning your PC for viruses

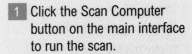

1 Click the Scan Computer button on the main interface to run the scan.

2 A scan may take some time, so you can use the Pause or Stop buttons to halt it for whatever reason. When you run the Scan Computer tool again, you'll be asked if you want to resume from an interrupted session.

3 When a scan is completed you will be shown the test result summary, telling you how many files were checked and whether it discovered any viruses.

3

Important

!

If a virus is found, you'll be offered the option to delete, fix, ignore or move it into quarantine (these are standard options that remain roughly the same across most anti-virus applications). False hits do happen, but don't choose to ignore something unless you're sure you know what the file is. Delete will obviously remove the file straight away while moving it into quarantine will stop it affecting your system but allow you to retrieve later if necessary. Fixing virus-infected files does not usually work but there's no harm in trying if the file is important.

Jargon buster

Quarantine – when referring to anti-virus and spyware applications, quarantine is where all the nasty programs get dumped. A protected area of the hard disk, security tools hold infected files in quarantine so that you can examine them later or restore them if necessary without them causing damage to your system.

Running a manual scan

▶

We're going to run another scan now, but instead of just clicking Scan Computer we're going to configure exactly where we want the software to look for viruses.

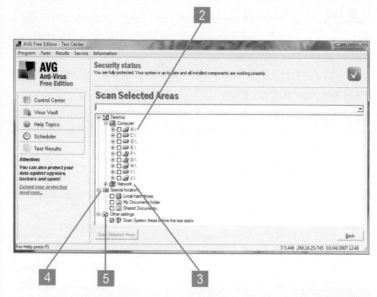

1 Choose Scan Selected Areas from the main interface.

2 Under the My Computer icon you'll see your hard drives, the most common place for a virus to infect your PC. You can choose which drives to scan by clicking the corresponding box.

3 If you're on a network you can scan the network drives or folders you have access to from your PC by clicking the '+' symbol to expand the My Network Places folder and ticking the relevant boxes.

4 Special Locations are areas on your hard drive that are most relevant to you, and are often places that you're most likely to find viruses in. If you have multiple users, you can scan the Shared Folders area in case infected files have been saved there unawares by other users of your computer.

5 The system areas of your hard drive are where the data essential for the day-to-day running of your PC is kept. Any problems here are likely to increase substantially if they lead to malicious infection. This box should always be ticked.

Timesaver tip

If you have a lot of data on your hard drive, or perhaps multiple hard drives attached to your system, you may find it takes a long time to scan everything for viruses. If you want to perform a faster scan for peace of mind, just choose the local hard drive – usually the C:\ drive, on which Windows is installed. This is far more likely to accumulate infections since the majority of files you'll be handling will be to and from this drive. Since Windows is run from this drive viruses that attack your operating system will also be nestling here if you're unlucky enough to attract any.

Jargon buster

Network Places – a central location in Windows that shows your networked drives and computers.

Installing antivirus software on your computer will help you stay virus-free but isn't enough protection against other Internet threats. Now that broadband is the norm for Internet users, it's more important than ever to ensure you're running a firewall to help prevent your computer being compromised. A firewall acts as a buffer between your computer and the rest of the world, and can analyse and filter content by comparing the inputs and outputs on your computer with a list of 'safe' web sites and computers. Here we'll be using the built-in Windows Firewall, which offers basic protection but is very simple to set up. You can buy specialist firewall packages but at the time of writing few are compatible with Vista, so double-check yours is before handing over any money.

Using Windows Firewall

1 Access the Windows Firewall by either opening the Security Centre or clicking Windows Firewall in the Control Panel.

2 Adjust the Windows Firewall settings by clicking this link.

3

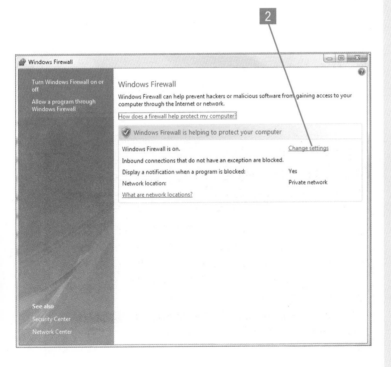

Using Windows Firewall (cont.)

3 By default the firewall should be on, if it's not and you have no other security software click here to enable it.

4 This option stops all incoming traffic to your computer, which is useful when you connect to an unknown or insecure network.

5 Disable the firewall. This is not recommended unless you have some other firewall software installed.

6 In the Settings window click Exceptions. These options allow you to deny or allow a program access to the Internet. New programs will cause Windows Firewall to ask whether you wish to allow the connection or stop the program communicating with the outside world.

7 Remove or add a check to the box next to a program to allow it access or stop all communications.

8 If you're unsure about one of the programs or services in the list, select it then click Properties for more information.

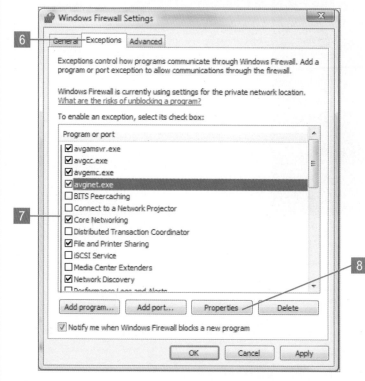

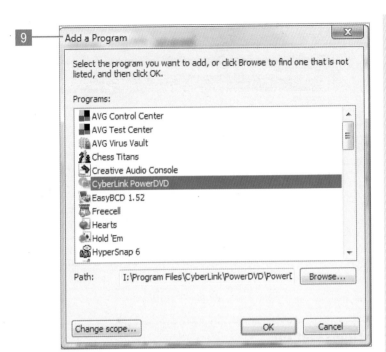

9 If a program is not visible in the list, click Add a Program, then scroll through the list of applications. Click Browse to select an application manually.

10 Connections are made through numbered ports and all programs use a specific port, or range of ports. If a program or service is being blocked and you know its port number, you can allow it manually. Click Add Port, enter a name for the new entry and then type in the port number and select either TCP or UDP protocol. If you're not sure of these details check the manual or contact the manufacturer of the software.

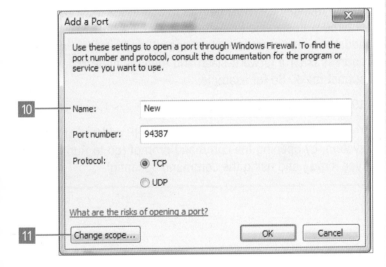

11 Click Change scope to set the source of network traffic. This allows you to block access to specific applications from the Internet, restricting it to just your local network.

3

Using Windows Firewall (cont.)

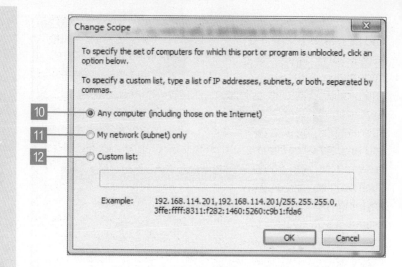

12 Select Any computer (which is the default option) to allow both local network and Internet access to this application.

13 Choose My network only to allow access only from computers on your local-wired or wireless – network. This prevents anybody from outside being able to use it.

14 Custom list allows you to enter the IP address of a single machine or a range of machines on your network. This then blocks both Internet and open network access, so only users on the systems listed will be able to communicate with that program.

Timesaver tip

If you have chosen the Custom list option it is possible to add multiple systems, but the IP addresses must be entered with specific formatting. Type in each IP address with a comma (but no space), and after the last address enter a forward-slash and then the network subnet mask. So for example:

192.168.1.2,192.168.1.3/255.255.255.0

You can find your subnet mask, and the IP address of a system, by opening the command prompt (go to Run, type 'cmd') and using the command 'ipconfig'.

Adware and Spyware are a growing concern for Internet users and as well as popping up annoying advertising and taking up bandwidth and processing time, can be used to gather information from your machine to report activities to advertising and product agencies looking to promote their services. Applications that you download and install may include adware or spyware and this is rarely flagged up in a noticeable fashion, so you may already have suspect software installed. Luckily, there are a range of programs around that will scan your machine for such problem files and give you the option to review and delete anything you don't like. With such a range of checkers and scanners available, it's often difficult to choose one to use. We've chosen Spybot Search & Destroy since, through tests, it has been proven to recognise and remove the widest range of problem files. The software is extremely easy to use and comes with update features to keep it abreast of the latest threats.

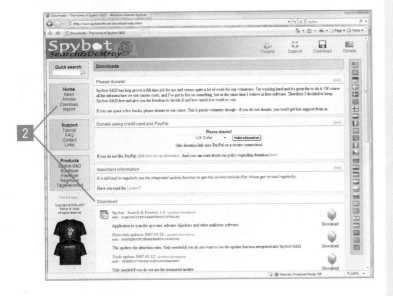

Protecting your system from spyware

1. First of all you'll need to download Spybot Search & Destroy from www.spybot.info so you can install it and run your first scan.

2. Click the Download link from the left menu, then click Spybot Search & Destroy from the list of software applications.

3. This will take you to a mirror page containing a number of links, click one and save the file to your computer. If the download is going slowly, cancel it and start again using one of the other file mirrors.

Jargon buster

Spyware – applications that monitor your computer and return data about your activities to the people who created them. Often combined with adware. Many spyware applications are malicious, intrusive and incredibly stubborn, proving extremely difficult to remove once they're into your PC. There is a thin line between spyware and a virus.

Jargon buster

Adware – installed along with other applications and delivers adverts through the application window or pop-up windows. Often, adware is more of an annoyance than a real threat, as many free programs use it to bring in money.

Installing Spybot

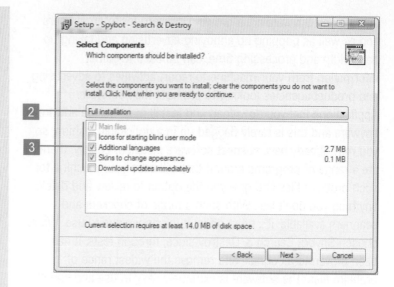

1 After you've saved the file to your computer from the Spybot website, locate the installer and double-click to run it.

2 During the process you'll have various options to configure. The installation types selected in the drop-down menu will quickly select common configurations. Full installation is the default and will include skins for changing the appearance, and additional languages as well as the default English text.

3 You can also tell Spybot to check for new updates when it connects and install some icons for blind user mode. Check and uncheck these options and other options as necessary to customise your installation.

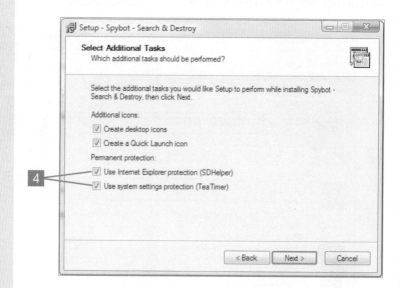

4 Spybot includes a number of additional utilities and you have the option of installing these with the main application. SDHelper protects Internet Explorer against malicious web code, while TeaTimer stops spyware planting its roots into Windows by alerting you to changes to the registry.

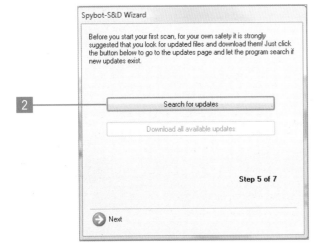

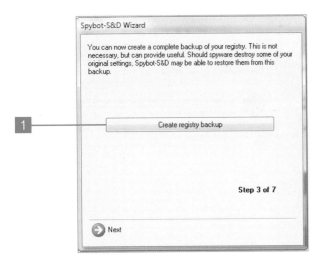

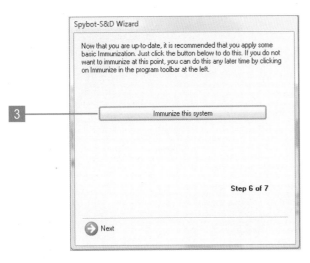

Configuring Spybot Search & Destroy

1 The first thing you'll see when starting Spybot after installation is a setup wizard that takes you through some essential steps to secure your system and prepare Spybot for use. Registry backup is important as it will restore Windows if any damage occurs.

2 You can also search for updates. Spybot will go online and check for the latest updates to its spyware definitions and the program itself.

3 Immunise is a useful option that secures your PC against some common threats by changing certain settings and blocking particular websites and applications.

3

Using Spybot Search & Destroy

1. Click the Search & Destroy button to scour your hard disk for that troublesome spyware.

2. If Spybot does something to your system that later causes problems use the recovery option to reverse the changes.

3. If you didn't do it during the initial setup, you can access the Immunise feature here as well. It also has an Undo option to revert to your original settings.

4. Update the Spybot application and its spyware definitions here.

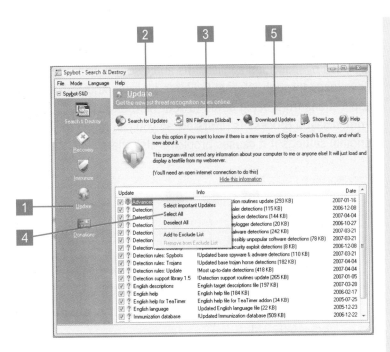

1 You should always ensure
Spybot has the latest spyware
definitions and core engine
updates to ensure protection
against new threats. To do this,
click the Update option.

2 To look for new updates click
Search for Updates.

3 If you get a checksum or
connection error when
updating, choose a new file
mirror from this menu.

4 New updates will be shown
here. You can click the check
box to select them individually,
or right-click and choose
Select All from the context
menu.

5 Once you've selected the
updates, click Download.

3

Immunising your system

By using the Immunise feature you can proactively stop some types of spyware. Immunise seals holes in your system that are used by malicious applications and also watches downloads through Internet Explorer, blocking known bad applications from being saved to your hard disk. The immunisation process is reversible so you can revert to your original settings if it causes problems elsewhere.

1. When you click Immunise from the main menu, Spybot will pop up a notice telling you whether you're protected against known threats already, or how many you are not protected against.

2. Click the Immunise button to protect your system. Immunisation typically only takes a few seconds.

3. Press check again to confirm that the Immunisation was successful and that you are protected.

4. Undo will reverse all changes made by the Immunisation.

5. Browser Helper protects you against online threats by watching for 'bad downloads' in Internet Explorer. Click the check box to enable or disable this feature.

6. Use the drop-down menu to change how Browser Helper will react when a download is detected. You can have it silently block the file, display a warning when a file is blocked or ask what you'd like to do with the download.

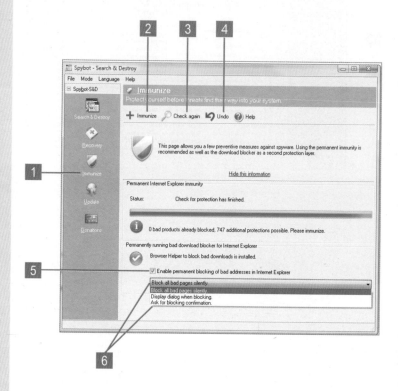

Timesaver tip

The Browser Helper feature only supports Internet Explorer. Users of Firefox, Opera and other web browsers will need to be a little more cautious, but in any case you should always have anti-virus software running. Every PC user should always scan files downloaded from the Internet with a virus program before running them or run the risk of catching a very nasty digital infection.

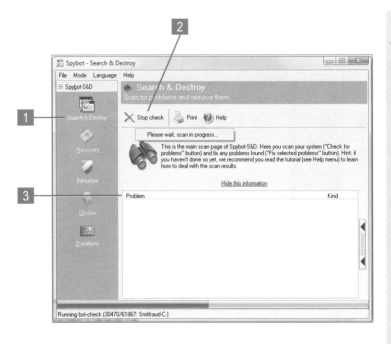

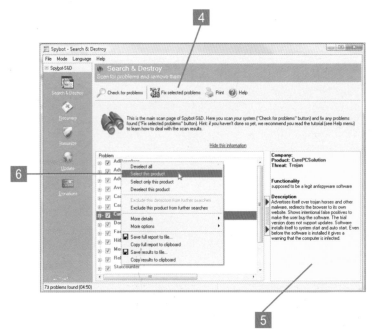

Scanning for spyware

1 Examine your PC for spyware by clicking Search & Destroy.

2 To begin a scan, press Check for problems. If you have checked for updates but not downloaded the new files you must complete the update process before it will run the scan.

3 As spyware is detected it will be displayed in the Problem window.

4 Once the scan is complete, the Fix selected problems button becomes visible. Select a problem from the list and click Fix to remove it from your system.

5 You can see more information about the spyware by expanding the description panel. Select something from the list and any information Spybot has about it will be shown, including relevant web addresses, notes and privacy policies.

6 Right-click in the Problem list for more options. Among other things you can select or deselect all detected spyware and save a scan report to a file or disk.

Security and privacy 101

Recovering deleted files

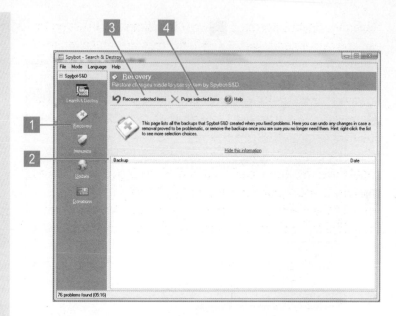

1. If you need to, some spyware files can be recovered after they're removed by choosing the Recovery option.

2. If Spybot has created any backups they will be listed here.

3. To recover, select a backup from the list and click Recover selected items.

4. You can clear the recovery list by clicking Purge. Once you've done this files will no longer be recoverable.

Generally, Spybot Search & Destroy is a simple application to use and understand, with its main features presented in an intuitive menu and containing plenty of instructions to ensure you never get lost. It does have some advanced settings, however, but these have been hidden away so as not to cause unnecessary confusion and to protect your system from potential damage that can occur with misuse. This doesn't mean you should be afraid to make use of them, but you should exercise some caution and read the included Help files carefully if you're not entirely sure. We'll take a brief look at some of the main options but it's well worth taking your time to explore the various extra features on offer.

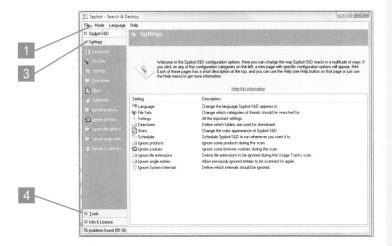

Important

Some software requires specific adware or spyware to be installed on your system for it to run properly, and will check for this software whenever you try and execute the program. For this reason, if you remove the adware or spyware the application may not run. There is rarely a way around this, as the software is specifically configured to run alongside the problem files. If you've removed the files, you may need to reinstall the application that needs them from scratch in order to run it successfully again. If you've quarantined the items you can restore them to regain access to that particular application.

Configuring Spybot's advanced options

1. Click the Mode menu and select Advanced Mode. A message will appear warning you that some options can potentially damage your computer. Click OK to continue.

2. Two new options will appear in the main menu.

3. Settings contains options for basic functions like language and skins to change the look of the program, but also provides the ability to customise the scanning process by excluding particular files or ignoring some programs.

4. Tools contains additional features that may be of use for protecting your PC, including a secure file shredder and controls for the TeaTimer application.

Exploring Spybot's Settings menu

▶

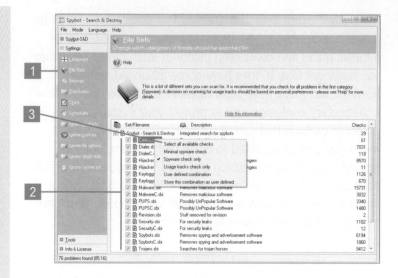

1 You can configure the type of files Spybot scans for with the File Sets option.

2 Click the check boxes to add or remove a file set from the scan.

3 Right-click to select all or choose from some pre-defined combinations. If you customise the sets, you can right-click and use Store this combination to save your selections.

4 Click Settings to view more options for Spybot. This section contains a vast number of general settings that affect the way Spybot behaves. You can remove or add desktop icons, configure automated scanning and setup automatic updates.

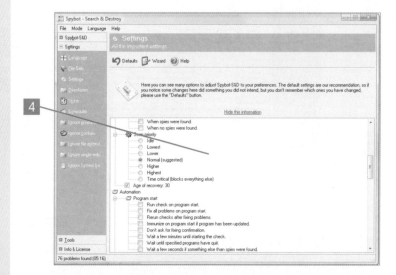

Exploring the Settings menu (cont.)

5 Another handy function found with the main Settings menu is the Scheduler, which lets you tell Spybot to automatically scan your PC at a particular time and day.

6 Click the Add button to add a new schedule task then press Edit.

7 The standard Windows schedule menu will appear. Go to the Schedule tab, choose when you'd like the scan to happen and click Apply.

8 The Schedule is now set. To delete it click the Remove button.

3

Using the Spybot tools

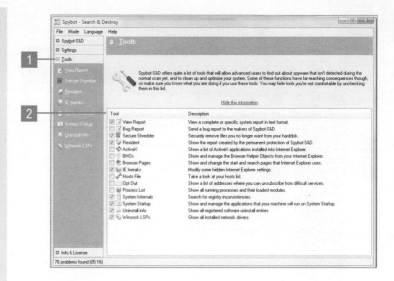

1. Click the Tools menu.

2. This section contains some utilities that can be damaging if not properly used. For this reason some of the options are hidden from view. Click the check boxes in the main window to add or remove them from the main Tools menu.

3. The Secure Shredder wipes files multiple times to make it difficult or impossible to recover them from your hard disk. If you have sensitive documents or other files you don't want others to discover this is useful for disposing of them.

4. Drag and drop files into the list, or right-click and choose Add to browse your hard disk.

5. Click the Templates button to add some common files to the shredder list.

6. Increase the number of shreds and it decreases the chance that a file will be recoverable.

7. When you're ready, click Chop it away!

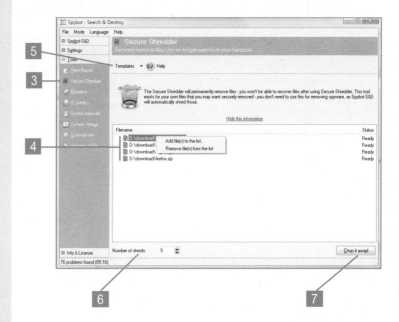

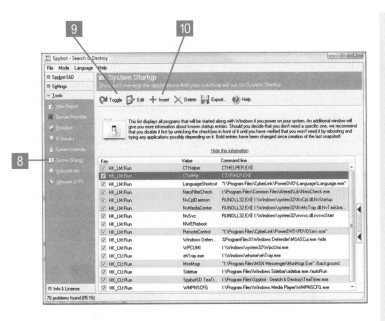

8 You can also use Spybot to control the programs that start with Windows. To do this click System Startup.

9 Click the check box – or click toggle – to disable/enable an application. Although you can delete a program from the list it's better to simply disable it in case there are problems the next time you switch on your PC.

10 You can make a new startup entry by clicking the Insert button. The program you choose will then load whenever you boot up Windows.

Protecting your system with passwords and encryption

Protecting your PC against external threats is only one part of security, and so far we've looked at how to do this with a firewall, virus scanner and by keeping adware and spyware at bay. What we haven't touched on yet is security for your PC against local threats, such as those posed by shared machines. Again, a range of software packages are around that offer you a variety of security services but we're using the WinGuard software for its ease of use and ability to protect a number of different areas of your system all from one interface. We'll be showing you how to use this software to prevent access to applications and various areas of your Window operating system, and how to encrypt sensitive files with your own personal passwords.

Get started with WinGuard

1. Go to www.winguard.com and download the latest version of the software. Save this to your computer and then run the installer.

2. WinGuard does not put an icon on your desktop, instead you must go to the WinGuard program group in the Start Menu and click Configuration.

3. You are required to enter a password each time you want to use the application. The default password is shown but you should change this to a password of your choosing the first time you run WinGuard.

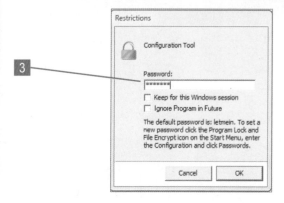

We've shown you how to set up individual user accounts to help restrict access to your files and folders, but there's no harm in adding extra security to keep sensitive data private. If you have a number of files or folders that you'd like to keep away from prying eyes, you can use an encryption service to make sure only you can open these files. You can also restrict access to other applications on your computer to prevent other users from changing your machine or using services or applications without permission.

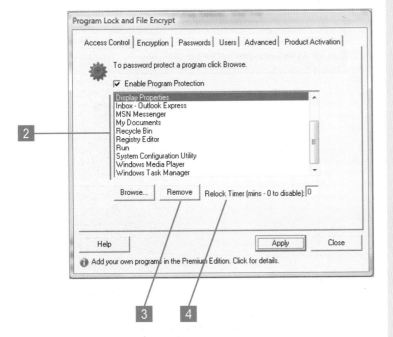

Password-protecting your applications

1 When WinGuard loads you'll be taken to the main menu. By default, program protection is disabled so click Password Protect a Program to begin.

2 Enable the program protection and every application listed will require a password to use. Typically, the most common ones you'll want to restrict are those that allow the user to make changes to the system, like the Control Panel or Run command.

3 Click Remove to delete a program from the list. Note however that the free version of WinGuard does not allow you to add programs, so to add a deleted item you would have to uninstall and reinstall WinGuard or enable the trial version to access the extra features.

4 Relock Timer automatically locks the listed applications after the set amount of time.

3

Password-protecting your applications (cont.)

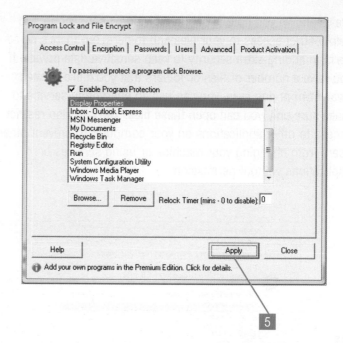

5 None of the changes you've made will come into place until you click the Apply button, at which point the chosen applications will be locked for access unless you have a password.

6 Open a program. You'll be greeted with the standard WinGuard password dialogue box. Type the password and your application will start.

One of the ways to protect files is by encryption, the conversion of data into a scrambled code, so that it cannot be read by normal means. Encrypted data must be unscrambled before it can be accessed. Most encryption is not completely foolproof but modern encryption techniques take a large amount of skill and computing power to crack.

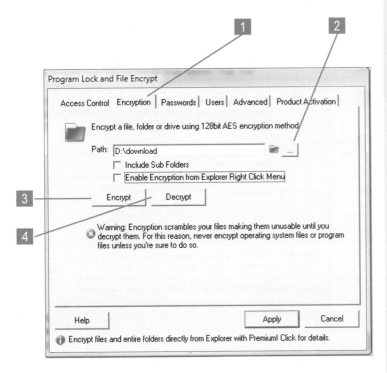

1 Choose the encrypt option from the main interface or go to the Encryption tab in the Users menu.

2 Click the three dots alongside the File or Folder box and browse to a folder on your hard drive that contains files you'd like to encrypt.

3

3 Choose the Encrypt button to encrypt the contents. After encryption you won't be able to open these files unless you decrypt them using the software.

4 Click the Decrypt button to remove encryption you've previously applied using the software so the files can be opened again.

!

Important

Usually the only files you'll need to encrypt on a personal computer are those you've created yourself. Be careful when browsing around for files to encrypt. If you select system files, modules or essential areas of your machine that Windows needs to be able to read in order to run with stability, you may have problems since your operating system is unable to read encrypted files.

Jargon buster

Encryption – the conversion of data into a scrambled code, so that it cannot be read on normal means. Most encryption is not completely foolproof but modern techniques takes a large amount of skill and computing power to crack.

Configuring user account settings

By default WinGuard applies the settings you select to every single user on your PC. This is the easiest option as it saves you doing the same thing over and over again, but if you do not want it to affect your user account you'll have to configure WinGuard on a per-user basis.

1 Click the Users option in the main menu or the Users tab in the Configuration window.

2 The default option is for global settings that apply the WinGuard Configuration you select to every user account. This is the easiest and quickest method of protecting your system.

3 For more flexibility select This user only. With this method you can configure individual security profiles, blocking specific users from specific applications, but it will require you to log in to each user account to set up WinGuard.

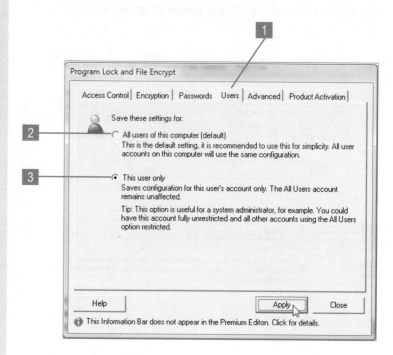

WinGuard uses a default password to allow you to access the configuration, but as it tells you this password each time the password prompt appears you must manually change it when you first use WinGuard. You can set separate passwords for protected programs, encrypted folders and access to the configuration menu. For the best security you should use a 'word' that includes a mix of numbers and letters.

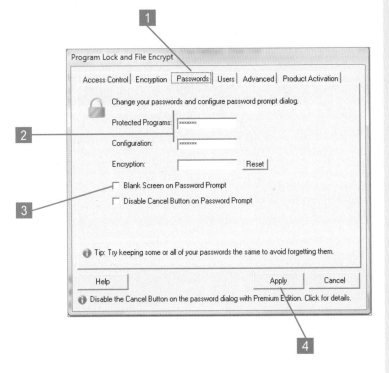

 Setting up a password

1 Click Passwords on the main menu or choose the Passwords tab.

2 Enter a new password in each field. A confirmation box will appear, so enter the same password again. It's best to enter a different password for programs, configuration and encryption.

3

3 Choose the blank screen option to blank out the display when the password prompt appears. The Disable Cancel Button option will not work until you enable the full trial version.

4 Click Apply to set the new passwords.

Setting up a password (cont.)

Important

Good password practice: password-protecting your computer, files and web sites is absolutely vital for protecting yourself against intruders, but it's all for nothing if you choose a password that's easy to break. Hackers use several methods to bypass security measures, and if you're aware of these you'll be better prepared. The simplest is just pure guesswork; if they know a little about you an obvious route is to try phrases you would find easy to remember such as the name of a pet, relative or favourite football team. They'll also try words which are commonly used as passwords, even blindingly obvious examples like 'password', '1234' or 'admin'. A more advanced technique is called a dictionary attack, which involves the use of a password cracking tool and a list of words. The program tries each word in the list until it finds a match. Brute force attacks attempt to guess a password by trying all possible combinations, but realistically these are far less likely to be successful, particularly if the attacker does not know how many characters the password contains.

Keep these methods in mind when choosing your passwords. The most important rules are to avoid using a word found in the dictionary, make the password as long as possible and always use a mix of letters and numbers, as well as punctuation when possible. To help you remember your password you can still use a memorable phrase, but adding the year that your dog was born or the score at the first football match you saw live to the beginning or end of a word will make it far more difficult to guess.

There are some areas of Windows that cannot be protected with the usual program protection feature. To stop users logging on to Windows or even running Windows Explorer you can use the advanced settings. This includes a feature that password-protects Internet Explorer downloads.

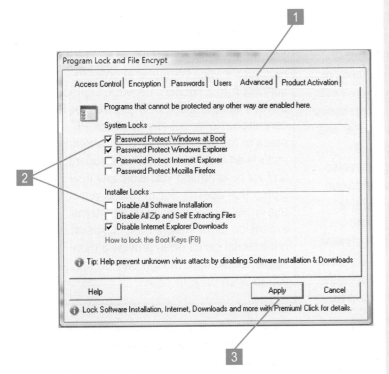

Configuring Winguard advanced options

1 Choose Advanced from the main menu or the Advanced tab in the Configuration screen.

2 To enable the advanced options check the boxes next to each. Be careful when using the Windows at Boot and Explorer options, because if you forget your password you won't be able to load Windows to uninstall WinGuard.

3

3 Press Apply and the settings will take effect. Some will not be noticeable until the next time you boot Windows.

Understanding wireless network security

Wireless networking is the most popular method of creating a network in the home thanks to its ease of use and convenience. While once we had to use lengths of networking cable to connect several computers, wireless networking replaces the wire with radio waves, sending your data over the air to any receivers in range. It is much easier to set up as all you need is a wireless router and receivers on each system, but the obvious downside is that anybody within range can also pick up that signal, and unless you secure your network they could access your data and use your Internet connection. This is illegal and people have already been prosecuted for stealing bandwidth, but it's very tempting for a neighbour to use your Internet service instead of paying for their own, and there are even people who drive around with laptops searching for insecure wireless networks. It presents a danger to you, because if someone were to access illegal content or use your connection for hacking and other illicit activities it would be traced back to your home.

This shouldn't put you off setting up a wireless network, however, all you have to do is take advantage of the features that are standard in every wireless router. Routers always include passwords that encrypt the data and stop other people from hopping onto your signal, simply look for the wireless security settings in your router configuration and enable either WEP or WPA security. WEP is not recommended unless it's the only available option, as it's already very easy to crack and will only stop people with no

Timesaver tip

You will need some manner of wireless receiver for your computer in order to connect it to a wireless network. Laptop owners can purchase USB receivers or PC card expansions, but any notebook PC made in the last couple of years should include an internal receiver as standard, and we recommend you avoid any new laptop that doesn't. For desktops you can use either a USB receiver or an internal expansion card. They're both inexpensive, but internal cards often provide a more stable connection, though they do require you to open up your case.

knowledge of computer security. WPA is more secure, and you should also use the MAC filtering settings whenever possible. This allows you to enter the unique MAC address of computers on your network into the router, preventing other systems from connecting. With both WPA (or WEP, if you have to) and MAC filtering enabled, your network will be safe from intruders and you can enjoy the convenience of this wire-free technology.

Jargon buster

Wireless network – a computer network that uses radio waves to transmit and receive data instead of network cables.

Managing software and files

Introduction

Anyone who was using computers back in the days of Windows 3.1 or DOS will remember the installation and uninstall routines, which generally involved copying all the files to the hard disk and then deleting them when no longer needed. Nowadays it's all automatic and we simply need to run the installation file and watch as the files are copied across, then run the uninstall procedure to remove them again. Windows even has a dedicated option for managing installed applications. In this chapter we'll take you through a sample install and uninstall procedure to demonstrate what's involved and also look at how you can manage the files on your hard disk by moving, copying and deleting them and creating new folders and shortcuts, as well as searching your computer for that hard-to-find data.

What you'll do

Install applications

Patch and update software

Remove applications from your PC

Add and remove Windows components

Change default programs

Open and modify files

Move and copy files

Delete files

Learn about Recycle Bin options

Create new files, folders and shortcuts

Search your computer

Timesaver tip

Before heading into the details of how to install, move and copy files, we will take the time to stress the importance of an organised and consistent filing system. Although there are sophisticated search features you can use, you don't want to be resorting to them every time.

Installing applications

Installing applications on a modern PC is, generally, a very simple process that involves clicking a few Next buttons and selecting some options. To demonstrate, we're going to step through the installation of WinZip, the popular file compression tool. Obviously it's not within the scope of this book to take you through every possible installation procedure you'll encounter, but generally speaking once you've seen one you've seen them all. Certain installations will be more complex of course, Microsoft Office, for example, includes the option of a custom installation whereby you can select which individual components are used, but even then it's relatively user-friendly.

Run the installation file

1. Locate the executable installation file (it will end in .EXE or .MSI) for the program you wish to install and double-click it to start. Programs on CD should start automatically when you place the disk in your computer.

2. You'll usually get a dialogue box or two introducing the program. In this example we click Setup to continue or Cancel to end the installation.

3. If it asks where you want to install the program, choose Browse to select an alternative location. The Program Files folder is the default for most recent applications. To make things simple it's best to keep all your applications in one place.

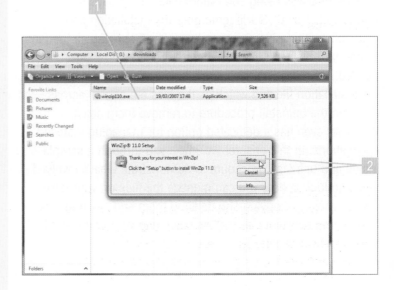

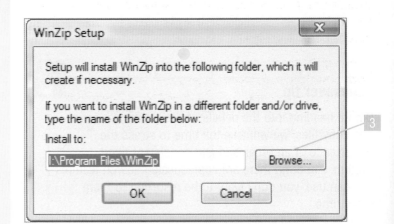

Jargon buster

Freeware – free software. Some have 'Pro' features that are unlocked by paying a registration fee.

EXE – a file with the .EXE extension means that it is an executable program file, a self-contained program that will run on its own. This can be a software installation package or application.

Extension – the letters after a filename that tell you what kind of data the file contains. For example '.jpg' is a JPEG image and '.txt' is a text file.

Shareware – trial software that can be used until a certain expiry date, at which point you must pay to continue using it.

For your information

The best place to find new software is of course the Internet, where there are thousands upon thousands of sites offering downloads of freeware and shareware. Freeware is free software that costs nothing to use. Often there will be a 'Pro' version of the tool which must be paid for but offers more features. Shareware is a term for trial programs. Sometimes they are unrestricted trials which must be purchased after a certain length of time; others have features that are disabled until you register.

Some of the most popular download sites are www.download.com, www.tucows.com and www.majorgeeks.com. You can download a free trial for WinZip from any of those sites or from its official homepage at www.winzip.com.

Did you know?

Don't fancy shelling out for the pricey Microsoft Office? OpenOffice (www.openoffice.org) is a free, open-source Office suite that includes a fully-featured word processor, spreadsheet, database and image editor. You can also play music and video files for free using Winamp (www.winamp.com) or edit images using the powerful and bizarrely named GIMP (www.gimp.org). All these are free alternatives to commercial applications. Just about any major program out there has a freeware clone, so if you're strapped for cash and in dire need of software this is one option. See the final chapter for more places to get great software.

4

Installing applications (cont.)

Read the license agreement

1. Before the installation begins you will almost always be shown a License Agreement, which lays out what you can and cannot do with the program. If you really don't agree with the terms, click No to cancel. Otherwise Yes will take you to the next step.

2. Click the Next buttons to continue through the installation. Some applications will start to install almost immediately while others, such as WinZip, include options like these asking you to select an interface style.

For your information

If you click No at the License Agreement dialogue box, the software will not be installed.

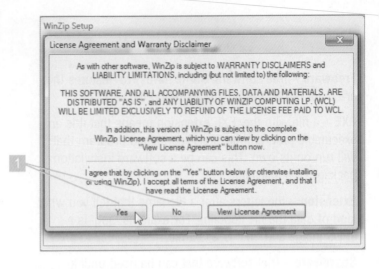

WinZip Setup

License Agreement and Warranty Disclaimer

As with other software, WinZip is subject to WARRANTY DISCLAIMERS and LIABILITY LIMITATIONS, including (but not limited to) the following:

THIS SOFTWARE, AND ALL ACCOMPANYING FILES, DATA AND MATERIALS, ARE DISTRIBUTED "AS IS", and ANY LIABILITY OF WINZIP COMPUTING LP. (WCL) WILL BE LIMITED EXCLUSIVELY TO REFUND OF THE LICENSE FEE PAID TO WCL.

In addition, this version of WinZip is subject to the complete WinZip License Agreement, which you can view by clicking on the "View License Agreement" button now.

I agree that by clicking on the "Yes" button below (or otherwise installing or using WinZip), I accept all terms of the License Agreement, and that I have read the License Agreement.

Yes   No   View License Agreement

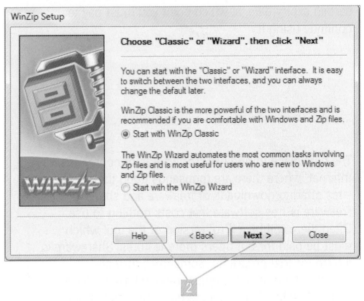

WinZip Setup

Choose "Classic" or "Wizard", then click "Next"

You can start with the "Classic" or "Wizard" interface. It is easy to switch between the two interfaces, and you can always change the default later.

WinZip Classic is the more powerful of the two interfaces and is recommended if you are comfortable with Windows and Zip files.

⦿ Start with WinZip Classic

The WinZip Wizard automates the most common tasks involving Zip files and is most useful for users who are new to Windows and Zip files.

○ Start with the WinZip Wizard

WINZIP

Help   < Back   Next >   Close

Jargon buster

License agreement – the legalese that appears whenever you install software and lays out exactly what you can and can't do with an application. For the average home user there's probably not much of relevance or interest. If you're planning on using a program in a business capacity however you might want to have a read as some free applications require business users to purchase a licence.

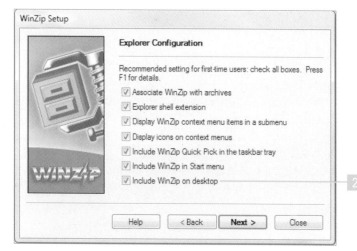

Choose an installation type

You'll sometimes be asked whether you want a custom installation or express installation. Express automatically configures the program using the most common settings, while Custom gives you full control over the installation steps.

If you've chosen the Custom installation you'll be able to customise the behaviour of the application during installation. With WinZip, this involves selecting whether you want a desktop and quick launch icon or Explorer extension, among others.

4

Timesaver tip

Although Custom installations are marked for 'Advanced Users', we'd recommend selecting this option whenever it is available. It gives you a far greater level of control over the way the program behaves, especially in regards to file associations and operating system integration. It can save you hassle later on especially when some programs don't make it entirely obvious how to reverse the choices made during installation.

Installing applications (cont.)

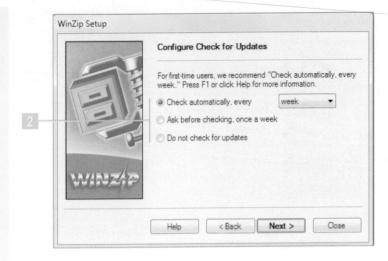

Complete the installation

1. If you chose to associate files with WinZip then you'll get the option of selecting which files are associated. For more information on file associations see the section on files later in this chapter. You can click Next to just accept the default selections for associations.

2. Some applications offer an update feature that goes online and searches for newer versions. During installation, WinZip gives you the choice of having the program check automatically for updates, ask for permission or never check. If you select the last option you can still manually check for new updates.

Important

Before running any software application you should always ensure it is free of viruses and other harmful software. Virus scanners should always be configured to manually scan files as they're accessed, but you can run a manual scan anytime you like and this will often be available as an option in the context menu if you right-click on a file. Spyware is also a risk. If the spyware is legitimate the company is required to ask you to 'opt-in' and agree to them installing it. Check the license agreement and installation options for mentions of additional software, especially web browser and desktop toolbars. Others will install spyware without permission. See the previous chapter for more information on viruses and spyware.

WinZip Setup

Other Options

Some WinZip features require optional external programs. You can configure these program locations now by clicking on Program Locations, or wait until you need them and choose "Configuration" from the "Options" menu and then click the "Program Locations" tab.

Program Locations...

☑ Create WinZip program group and icons

☐ Create icon for WinZip Self-Extractor Personal Edition

| Help | < Back | **Next >** | Close |

Installing applications (cont.)

3 You have a few final options to select before the installation is complete. Click the Program Locations button to configure external applications for handling file types WinZip does not recognise. Many applications will ask you to do this, often to specify a virus scanner.

4 Once the installation process is finished your program is ready to run. You can find your application either via a shortcut in the Quick Launch bar, Start menu or on the desktop, depending on the options you chose during installation, or you can navigate to the directory where its files are stored.

4

Patching and updating software

Patches are a necessary evil when using a PC. It can be a pain to constantly ensure that every one of your programs is up-to-date but it's absolutely vital for ensuring the security and smooth running of your system. It's not all bad, either, as some patches aren't always used to fix holes but to give your program new features. Some require you to download a newer version of the installation file while others can be patched either automatically via a central server or by downloading a small patch file that is simply run and installed like any other program.

1 Some programs, such as WinZip, can be updated by downloading the newer version and installing it over the top of the previous one. Doing this should usually retain important details like registration keys and settings. If your program is several versions old however, it may be a good idea to uninstall it before installing the update. In our example, we have updated WinZip by installing the latest version, available on the WinZip homepage.

2 A patch will update certain parts of the application without requiring you to do a complete reinstall. They are most often used for large commercial packages where it's not possible or unrealistic to download a complete new version of the program. Here, we're applying a security patch to Microsoft Office, downloaded from Microsoft's Windows Update site.

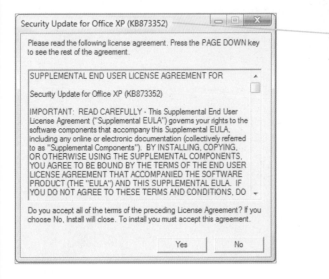

Many applications will communicate with a central server to inform you about new updates. It's a good idea to enable this option or allow the program to connect to its server since you'll be alerted to critical security updates. Many programs have holes that are discovered and fixed later on, so, as well as making sure you've got the latest features, software patches will help keep your system secure.

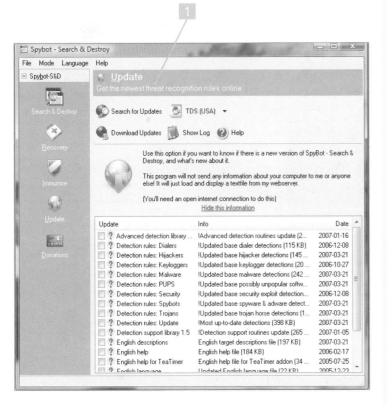

Use live update

1. The easiest way to update software is using live or auto-update functions, if they're available. These will connect to a server, download the latest updates and install them without you needing to do much at all. We've used anti-spyware tool Spybot, which can download new updates to its definition files without needing a reinstall.

4

Jargon buster

Auto-update – software that auto-updates will download and install the latest version of itself, often without user-intervention. Sometimes called a live update.

Removing applications from your PC

Once you no longer need an application, you should remove it from your system to save hard disk space. All applications with an install procedure will (or should) make it simple to remove them when you're done. Programs and features, in the Control Panel, is the central location for uninstalling programs. Once a program is installed it will be listed in this where it can be uninstalled or modified. Programs and features also contains options for changing the default applications for web browsing, email and other tasks and making changes to Windows tools and features.

1 Open up the Control Panel, click Classic View, then open Programs and Features.

2 In Programs and Features you have several tasks down the left-hand side. View installed updates displays all updates to the Vista operating system.

3 This link takes you to the Windows Marketplace website where you can purchase and download new programs.

4 All programs downloaded from the Marketplace can be found in the digital locker.

5 Click this option to enable/disable certain services and features.

6 All installed applications are listed here (provided they have registered themselves with the system). The column on the far right displays the amount of space a program uses on your hard disk.

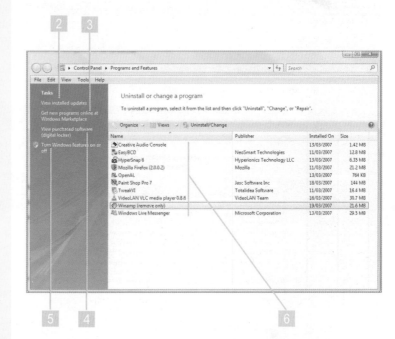

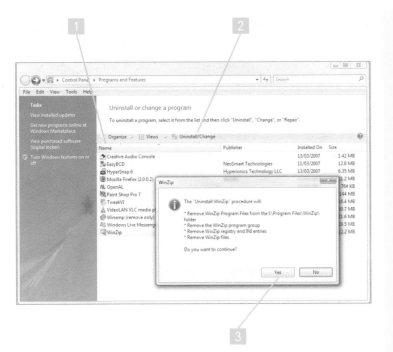

Removing applications from your PC (cont.)

Remove applications

1 Scroll down the application list and click the program you want to remove.

2 Click Uninstall/Change to begin removing the selected application from your computer.

3 A dialogue box will appear confirming that you want to remove the program, or sometimes asking if you wish to make changes to the installation. If you uninstall, a progress bar will show the application being deleted, followed by a confirmation. The steps can vary, however, and you may be asked to select some options along the way or be prompted to confirm the removal of system files.

Important

Sometimes the uninstall procedure will become corrupted and you'll be unable to remove a program through the Programs and Features option. In this situation you may be able to do it simply by locating the uninstall file in the program directory and running it; they're often named 'uninstall.exe' or some variation thereof, as it could be that Windows just cannot find the uninstall file itself. If this also refuses to work you can just delete the program folder. It would be a good idea however to move this into the Recycle Bin until you're sure you no longer need it, rather than completely deleting the files, just in case you encounter problems from Windows or other applications later on. Be aware that this will probably leave references to the application in the Windows Registry and if you want to completely remove these you will need to do it manually by searching the Registry.

Adding and removing Windows components

1. Open the Control Panel and go to Programs and Features.

2. Click Turn Windows features on or off from the Tasks list. Using these controls you can easily add or remove some Windows components and applications.

3. To remove a feature that's installed, simply uncheck the box beside it, and vice versa to install. Click OK to finalise the process.

Previous versions of Windows gave you little assistance in changing the default applications used by the system to open particular file types or perform certain functions. Windows Vista greatly improves on this by offering a wide range of easy-to-use controls for handling file associations. You can quickly change the associations for certain tasks like web browsing by using the Program Access and Defaults interface that was first seen in Windows XP, or customise the settings of specific applications with the new default programs configuration.

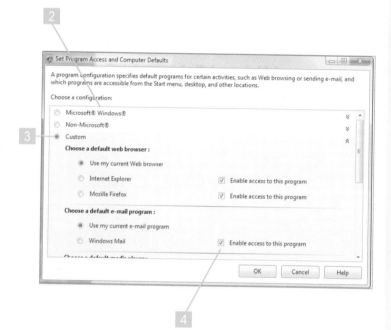

Changing default programs

1. Open the Start menu and click Default Programs, then choose Set Program Access and Defaults from the menu.

2. If you want to use only Microsoft products, select Microsoft Windows and click OK. To use non-Microsoft products, select that option. This will depend on programs being compatible with that function.

3. The Custom option allows you to select exactly which programs are used. If an application is compatible with the Program Access function it will appear as an option in the list, otherwise you can use the Windows default or the current application.

4. If you don't want a program to be available in Windows, uncheck the Enable access box next it. This will remove links to the program on the desktop and Start menu.

Changing default programs (cont.)

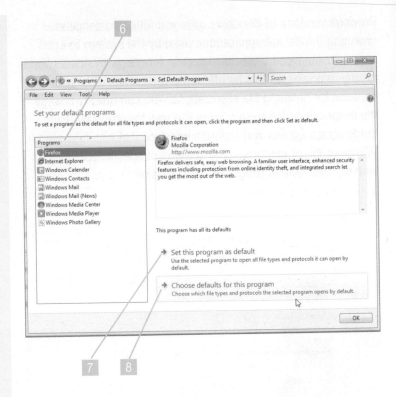

5 To customise the file handling of specific applications, go back to the Default Programs menu and select the Set your default programs option.

6 Select a program from the list.

7 Choose Set this program as default to use it as the default application for all the file types that program supports. This will overwrite any previous file associations.

8 If you want more control, click Choose defaults. This will allow you to individually modify the behaviour of every supported file type for the selected application.

All common files in Windows will, or should, be associated with a program, meaning that if you open them they will always be viewed by that particular application. You can of course change this file association or just open a file once with an alternative program. All of this can be done very quickly and easily by opening the context menu on a file. You can also apply attributes, like making a file hidden or read-only, which will help stop them being overwritten or deleted because in most cases the computer should ask you before running any action on a read-only file.

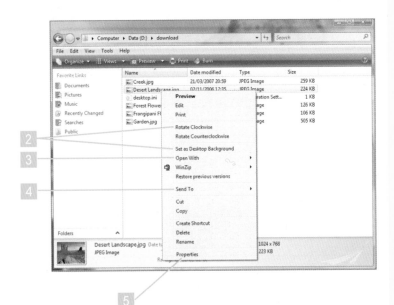

Use file execution and view options

1 Right-click on a file to bring up the context menu. The options that are shown will change depending on the file type.

2 We've clicked on a picture, so the context menu includes the relevant commands for image files. Vista includes new options to rotate an image without opening an image editor and you can also set the picture as your desktop background. If you install any image viewers or editors it's likely they'll add new commands for pictures into the context menu.

3 Use the Open With menu to use a program other than the default application associated with that file.

4 Use Send To when you wish to transfer the file to another part of your system or send it over the Internet.

5 You can view the file attributes by clicking the Properties option. This shows you information such as the file size, creation and modification dates and allows you to set options such as Read Only.

Opening and modifying files (cont.)

Run files with the Open With menu

1. Right-click on a file and select the Open With menu. This allows you to run the file with an alternative application from the list.

2. Click Choose Default Program and you can select another program from your hard disk.

Run the file with another application

1. The Recommended Programs list shows applications that Windows already associates with the selected file.

2. Other Programs shows other applications registered on your system, they may not necessarily be able to open the file.

3. Click Browse to select another program from your hard disk.

4. If you want to change the file association so that the file will always open with the program you choose, tick Always use the selected program.

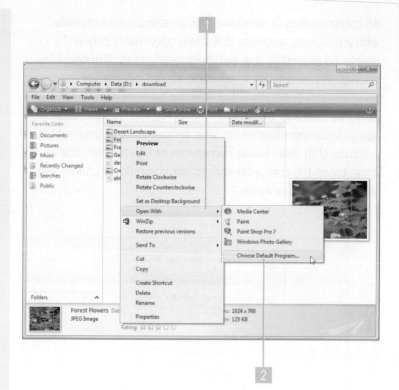

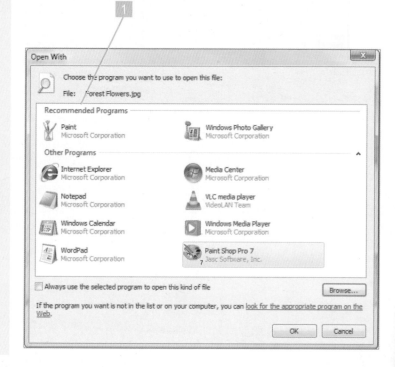

Moving files around the system is incredibly simple, just a case of dragging and dropping them into new locations. You'll want to do this to keep your files organised but remember not to touch important system files and folders. If you attempt to move any system or read-only files Windows should usually warn you beforehand. Unless you know what you're doing it's best to leave them be.

Dragging and dropping files from one folder to another on the same drive will automatically move them. Doing it from one drive to another will copy the files.

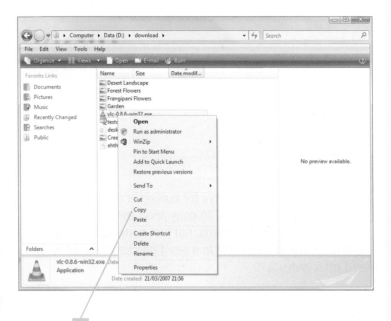

Moving and copying files

Copy and move files between folders

1 You can move a file by dragging and dropping it into another folder.

2 Or, right-click on a file and select Cut or Copy, then right-click in the new folder and choose Paste. Note that files copied into the same directory as the original will automatically have 'Copy of' added to the file name.

4

Moving and copying files (cont.)

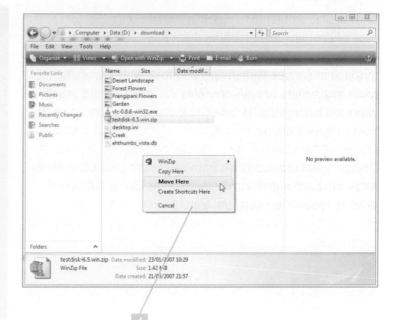

3　Move and copy groups of files by selecting them with the normal method and then using the Cut and Copy options.

4　You can also drag and drop with the right mouse button. When you release the button a Context menu will appear with Copy, Move and Create Shortcut options. This is quicker than using the right-click Cut and Copy options.

Timesaver tip

Remember the shortcut keys for cutting and copying. Press Ctrl+X to cut, Ctrl+C to copy and Ctrl+V to paste. This works in most programs, not just copying files, e.g. you can cut and paste text in a word processor, or copy text off a website.

Once files are no longer required you should delete them from your system to free up hard disk space and reduce clutter. By default, Windows places deleted files in the Recycle Bin and this is something that many people don't learn until later on, when they've used up all the space and find several useless gigabytes sat in there. You can help your PC run smoothly by emptying the Bin on a regular basis or whenever it gets too full. Don't forget that it does actually have a purpose, though, because if you accidentally remove a file and place it in the Bin, it can be restored without any loss of data. If you're not bothered about this, you can delete files for good with a shortcut key or configure the Recycle Bin to always delete files immediately.

Deleting files

Move files to the Recycle Bin

1 By default, the Delete command will move files to the Recycle Bin. Select the file(s) and press the Delete key, or right-click and choose Delete, or drag and drop files into the Recycle Bin.

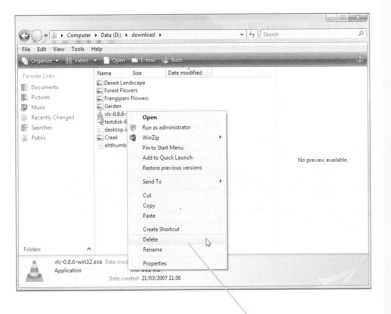

4

Timesaver tip

Hold down Shift and press Delete to bypass the Recycle Bin and delete a file straight away.

Deleting files (cont.)

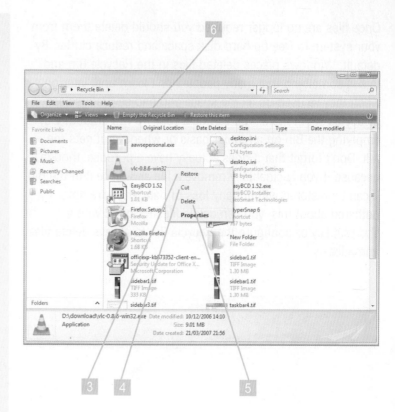

Use the Recycle Bin

2 Right-click on a file or group of files to bring up the options.

3 Choose Restore to put the file back in its original location on your hard disk.

4 Use Cut to move the file out of the Recycle Bin without restoring it to its original folder. You can then paste it to any location on your drive.

5 Once you're sure you no longer need a file, choose the Delete option or press the Delete key on your keyboard. This will remove the file from your computer.

6 You can clear the entire Recycle Bin by choosing Empty the Recycle Bin. This will delete every file at once.

Recycle Bin Properties

Recycle Bin Location	Space Available
Backup (E:)	111 GB
Data (D:)	239 GB
Local Disk (I:)	69.2 GB
Main (C:)	139 GB

Settings for selected location

○ Custom size:
  Maximum size (MB): 14318

○ Do not move files to the Recycle Bin. Remove files immediately when deleted.

☑ Display delete confirmation dialog

OK   Cancel   Apply

1 Right-click on the Recycle Bin and choose Properties. Notice the Empty Recycle Bin option, which allows you to empty the bin without opening it.

2 Check the Do not move files to Recycle Bin option to delete files from your hard disk without them going to the Recycle Bin. Be careful when using this because once a file is deleted it can be difficult to recover.

3 Enter a number to set the maximum amount of space, in megabytes, that the Recycle Bin will use on each drive.

4 Uncheck the Delete Confirm option to delete files immediately without a warning prompt. It's probably a good idea to leave this setting as is unless you have a very specific reason for it to be disabled.

Important

When you delete a file from Windows in the normal way, it isn't actually completely destroyed. What happens is that the operating system marks the space the file occupies as available, so that the next time data is written to the drive the old data could be overwritten. Even then, fragments of files can be retrieved using advanced techniques. From a security standpoint, this makes removing sensitive files a complete nightmare and experts will tell you that if data is of life or death importance, you should take the hard disk, dismantle it and then smash the pieces. Home users shouldn't need to go to those extremes however as there are a large number of file shredding applications which overwrite data multiple times and fill the gaps with junk information to make it harder to find. It won't stop dedicated police forensic units but if you sell your hard disk it will ensure that the new owner can't recover anything you've deleted. File shredders can be found on download sites or are included as part of packages like Symantec's Norton SystemWorks.

Creating new files, folders and shortcuts

Creating new files and folders is easy, just use the right-click Context menu and select the type of object you want. This is a quick way to create a new document or compressed zip file, for example, or a new folder. If you're handling lots of files, you can make life easy by using a bit of organisation and just creating folders to keep them grouped and organised.

Create a new file or folder

1. Right-click to bring up the Context menu, then go to New.

2. On a clean installation of Windows, you will have the option to create a new folder, shortcut or several new file types, such as a text file.

3. As you install applications, shortcuts for them will be added to the New menu. For example, we can create a new WinZip file without opening the WinZip application.

4. Just click on the item you want to create and it will appear in the current folder. Type in a new name for the file or hit Enter to leave the default filename as it is.

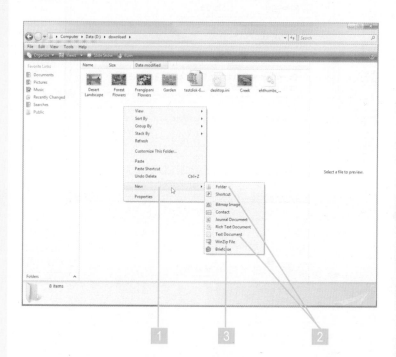

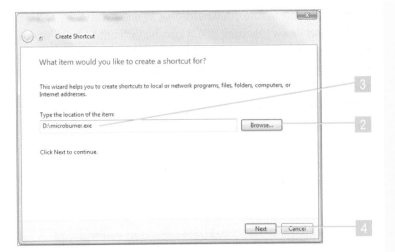

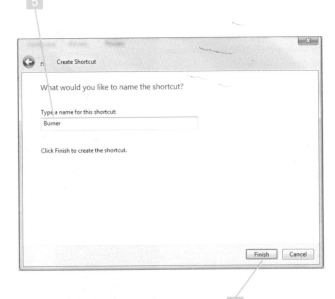

Make a shortcut

1. Go to the New menu as before, but this time select New Shortcut.

2. Click Browse and navigate to the location of the program you wish to shortcut.

3. The full program location will appear in the box.

4. Click Next.

5. Now type in a name. By default it will use the name of the program file with an .EXE extension. Call it something that you'll easily recognise.

6. Click Finish and the shortcut will be created.

4

Timesaver tip

If you want to quickly rename a file or folder, click once to select it, then once again on the text and the name will become an input box. If the file extension is visible be careful not to delete that otherwise Windows may not be able to recognise the file. You can however change the extension if you wish.

Using the indexed Search

It won't be long before your hard disk is filled with files and folders and when this happens it can be difficult to track down a particular file unless you're extremely organised. To assist you in locating errant data you can use the Windows search function. Vista's built-in search is a huge leap forward over Windows XP as it now indexes your hard drives, storing the location of files and programs and greatly reducing the time it takes to search your computer. A basic search function is now available on the Start menu, or you can open a fully-featured search application with a range of options.

Find files and folders on your PC

1. Open the Start menu and you'll see the search box in the lower part of the menu.

2. Start typing in the file, folder or application you're looking for and you'll notice that the search changes to match the characters. You may only need to enter a partial search term to locate the item.

3. Click Search from the Start menu to open the full-blown search program.

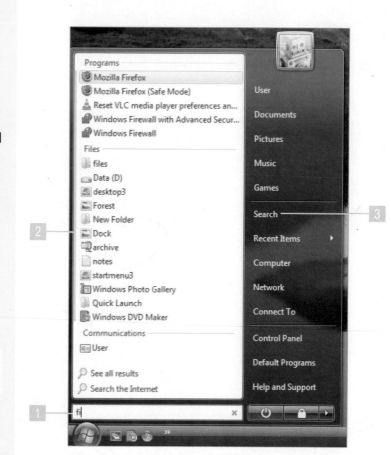

Timesaver tip

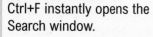

Ctrl+F instantly opens the Search window.

Using the advanced search options

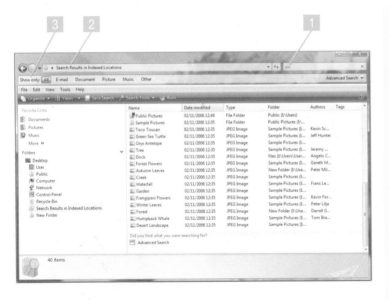

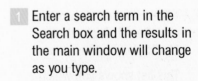

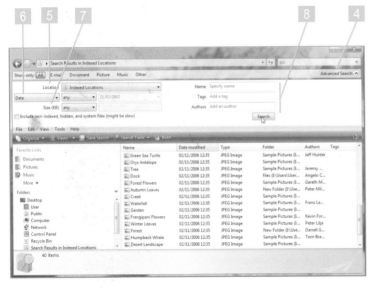

1. Enter a search term in the Search box and the results in the main window will change as you type.

2. By default it will search in indexed locations. You can select a specific drive or folder by clicking this drop-down menu.

3. Filter the result by choosing one of these options.

4. Click Advanced Search to reveal more search options.

5. Click here to search indexed locations or specific folders.

6. Search on, after or before a specific date.

7. You can also search by file size, either for an exact match or files that are bigger or smaller.

8. Vista allows you to tag photos with keywords and add other information to make them easy to organise and locate. Using the search you can find all tagged images matching criteria you choose.

Timesaver tip

When you run a Search or anything involving large numbers of files, many programs will allow you to use wildcards to automatically include large groups of files. Placing a wildcard in front of an extension would cover every file of that type, while placing a wildcard in the extension would search for every file type with that exact name.

Adjusting indexing options

1. Within the Search window click Search Tools, then Modify Indexed Locations.

2. This list shows you which folders and drives are currently being indexed by the search.

3. Click Advanced to access search options.

4. To add or remove locations for indexing click Modify.

5. To add or remove a location for indexing, check or uncheck the box next to a drive or folder. Click the arrows next to the icons to view subfolders.

6. The summary window will reflect the changes as you select new folders.

7. When you're finished click OK to apply the changes. The selected locations will be included the next time files are indexed.

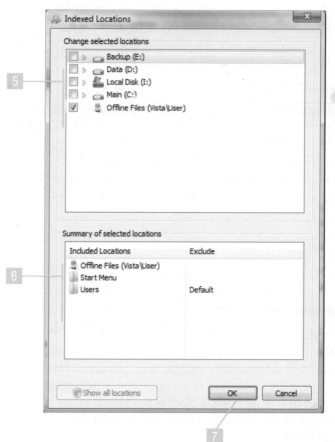

5

Hardware

Introduction

In the first chapter we gave you an overview of each component and its role, here we're going to show how you can perform a few of the most common upgrades. You're not going to be diving straight inside a brand new system the moment you get it, but eventually you'll want or need to open it up and make some changes to the innards. As your needs change and new software is released, you'll want more memory, hard disk space or graphical processing power, all of which is very easy to achieve by removing the old, plugging in the new and (sometimes) installing new drivers. Performing simple upgrades yourself takes very little time and can save you money where computer stores would charge for labour on top of parts, for a job that could take less than a few minutes. Modern systems are, in general, incredibly easy to build and maintain once you've got compatible parts, slotting together like expensive, electronic building blocks. You do need to be careful when handling components as they can be easily damaged by rough treatment and static discharge, but this is avoided simply by following a few basic safety rules. Once you've learnt the basics you could even start thinking about building your next system, which gives you total control over the quality of the hardware used, saves money and is incredibly satisfying once your new home-made PC is up and running.

What you'll do

Install a new graphics card and drivers

Change your graphics card settings

Upgrade your memory

Install a new hard disk

Use Disk Management

Change drive settings

Create multiple partitions

Install a new CD or DVD drive

Manage your hardware with Device Manager

Installing a new graphics card

If you're planning on just using your PC for office tasks, it's unlikely you'll ever need to touch the graphics card. If however you want to dabble in video, graphics editing or gaming then a new card is a possibility or even a necessity, especially if your system only came with a weak onboard or budget model. Fitting a card is usually pain-free, with the only problems coming from fiddly slot catches or outdated drivers. One very important thing you must check however is that any new card you buy is compatible with your motherboard. Newer motherboards use the new PCI-express interface standard while slightly older systems take AGP. Neither is compatible with the other, so check that you don't buy a PCI-express card for your AGP system. You'll also need to ensure that your power supply unit is properly equipped to handle the card. The very latest models use a great deal of power so a good 400W power supply is recommended, but you also need to ensure that you have a spare Molex power cable or, in the case of PCI-express cards, a six-pin PCI-e power connecter. Don't rush out to buy a new PSU if yours doesn't have the six-pin connection though, because most cards should include an adapter and if not, they can be purchased for a small amount from computer suppliers.

Important

If you've got an on-board graphics card (you'll know, because the monitor port will be alongside the other connections on the back of the motherboard and there'll be no graphics card in an expansion slot) you will need to disable this to use your new card. Enter your PCs BIOS (usually done by hitting the Del key when the PC first starts, though the methods can vary – consult your mother-board manual) then find the Integrated Peripherals section. There you should find an entry for on-board graphics. Disable it completely, then save and exit.

Jargon buster

AGP – Accelerated Graphics Port, based on the PCI interface, AGP was developed exclusively for graphics cards, replacing the general-use PCI slot. It's now being phased out in favour of PCI-express, but AGP cards are still being manufactured because of the abundance of AGP systems.

Anti-static bag – components are usually shipped in grey plastic bags that have been treated to protect against static damage. It's a good idea to hold on to these as they may come in useful when upgrading.

3

Installing a new graphics card (cont.)

Remove the previous card

1. Before you do anything else, go into Programs and Features and uninstall your current graphics card drivers. Shut down the system once that is finished.

2. If you already have a graphics card in the AGP or PCI-express slot, you'll obviously need to remove it first.

3. If the card has an extra power cable attached, carefully unplug this. The 6-pin PCI-express power connectors have a small catch that you'll need to press down on to release them.

4. The card bracket will be secured to the case in some way, usually with a screw though sometimes there is a tool-free mechanism. Release this so the card is loosened.

5. You'll now need to flick the slot catch which holds the card in place. Just press down on it until the back of the card pushes upwards. Some boards may have a slightly different mechanism, like a sliding catch, but these are quite rare.

6. Carefully lift the card out the slot and place it somewhere safe, preferably in an anti-static bag within a sturdy box.

Jargon buster

BIOS – Basic Input Output System, the software that enables basic functionality of hardware on all systems, whether they have an operating system or not, and allows you to configure hardware settings. The BIOS is stored on a Read-Only Memory (ROM) chip on the motherboard, so will always be available even if the hard disk crashes. You can access your BIOS by hitting the assigned key when your system starts, which is usually Delete.

PCI – Peripheral Component Interconnect, the most common type of interface found on PC systems now, it still appears on the very latest PCI-express boards to support expansion hardware like sound cards, which have yet to switch to using PCI-express.

PCI-Express – the 'sequel' to PCI and AGP interfaces, PCI-express offers a (potentially) huge increase in bandwidth. Newer motherboards include one or two PCI-e slots specifically for graphics cards and several more for additional expansion cards, alongside a couple of standard PCI slots.

5

Installing a new graphics card (cont.)

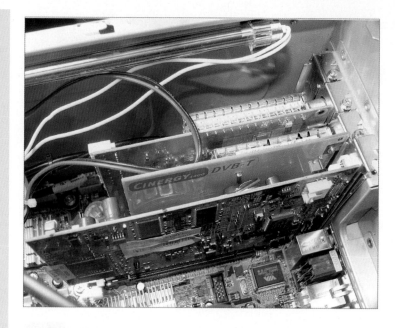

Install the new card

1 Simply put, you need to do the opposite of the previous steps. First make sure the slot catch is pushed all the way back.

2 Carefully and gently push the new card into the slot. Make sure that the lower part of the bracket slips between the back of the case and the motherboard and doesn't get caught.

3 Once the card is in the correct position, push firmly down on it until the slot catch clicks into place. Check that it's properly seated; it should be able to wiggle from side to side but not lift at the back.

4 Now secure the bracket to the case. Your card should be firmly fixed into place so that there's no movement and no possible chance of it coming loose when you plug in the monitor.

5 If additional power is required, use the appropriate power connection on the rear of the card, Molex for AGP and six-pin for PCI-express.

Important !

Hardware is extremely sensitive to static; you won't even know you've killed that brand new RAM module until your system refuses to start, so always take precautions when handling components. Use an anti-static wristband (available from computer stores) or if that's not possible, regularly touch a grounded metal object to discharge any static build-up. Avoid working on carpet; lino or wooden floors are preferable. RAM, CPUs and graphics cards are particularly sensitive and also some of the most expensive parts, so always exercise extreme caution when handling these components.

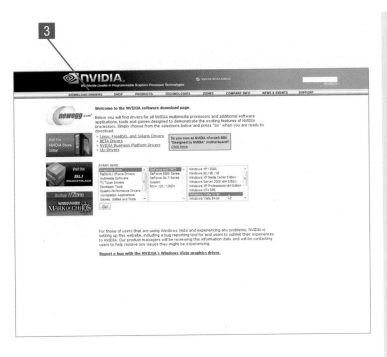

3

Installing the graphics card drivers

1 Once you reboot with your new card you will need to install the drivers in order for it to work properly. Windows will display – but only in a lower resolution.

2 Windows will tell you it has found new hardware, click cancel, we don't want it to install any other software.

3 If you have a driver CD, insert that and it will start automatically, just follow the prompts to install. Otherwise, you will need to download the drivers off the manufacturer's website. NVIDIA card owners should go to www.nvidia.com while ATi's site is www.ati.com.

4 Run the install routines and follow the installation steps, they are straightforward and once finished will reboot your system.

Important

You should check regularly to see that your graphics card drivers are up-to-date, since newer versions will offer improved performance, stability and features.

5

Changing your graphics card settings

Both NVIDIA and ATi, manufacturers of the most popular graphics cards, provide numerous options for their cards with the driver software. Although you do not need to change these settings to use the card, they do offer an extra level of control. We're going to take a look at NVIDIA's Control Panel as an example, but the software from both companies is accessed in the same way and offers similar options.

Open the graphics card controls

1 Right-click on the desktop and choose NVIDIA Control Panel. ATi users will have a similar option.

2 You can also access some basic graphics settings via the Personalise menu, where you can adjust the resolution, manage multiple displays and use advanced functions like colour management.

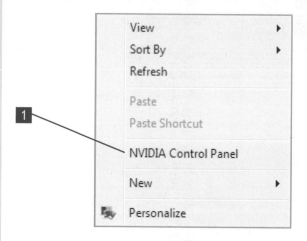

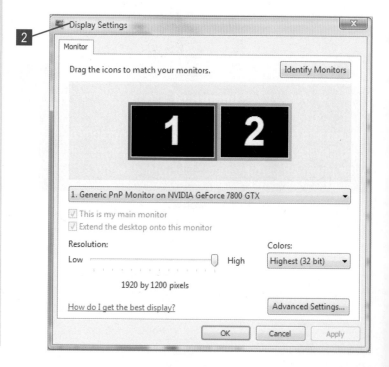

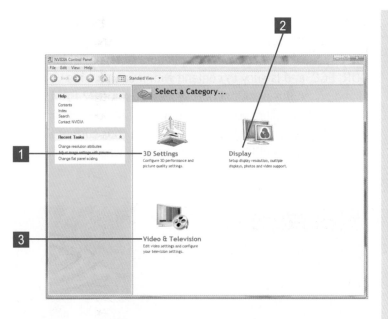

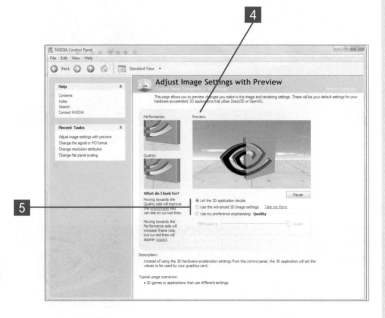

Use the Control Panel

1 The Control Panel gives you three main categories to adjust settings. 3D settings allows you to adjust the graphics for quality or speed.

2 Display is used to manage aspect ratios, multiple monitors, colour settings and other related options.

3 Video and Television is used to adjust the input settings for different types of connectors when using external video hardware.

4 If you click 3D Settings you'll see a preview window that allows you to check how the settings will affect your graphics.

5 You can choose whether you want the graphics to be adjusted by each application, or manually select quality or performance using either the advanced options or the slider.

5

Upgrading your memory

Certainly one of the easiest upgrades you can perform, the biggest hurdle you've got when upgrading memory is ensuring you buy the correct type. With a plethora of technical terms DDR, ECC, and latency to contend with it can become incredibly confusing. Most new systems use DDR2 RAM, but you'll need to ensure you get the right speed. Consult your motherboard manual, check the sticker on your current RAM modules or contact the supplier to find out what type of memory you require.

Remove the old memory

1 Locate the two catches on either end of the RAM slot and push them down. The module will rise out of the slot, gently lift it out and place it in an anti-static bag for safe-keeping.

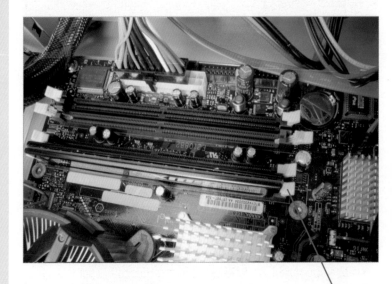

Important

RAM is incredibly sensitive to static. When handling it take care not to touch the gold contacts or chips, hold it by the edges whenever possible and take the usual precautions against static build-up.

1

2

Upgrading your memory (cont.)

Insert the new memory

1 Line up the notches in the RAM modules with the slots on the motherboard and carefully slide them into place.

2 Once you're sure that they're in the right position, push firmly until the catches either end click into place. It shouldn't require much force, so if you feel a lot of resistance double-check that the modules are definitely lined up properly.

3 That's it! Boot up your system and watch during the POST as the memory is counted and checked. No drivers are needed.

Jargon buster

Intel – the largest manufacturer of central processing units in the world. The US giant had a monopoly on the CPU market until AMD introduced the Athlon series processor.

Important

If you're buying two or more RAM modules, for example two 512 MB sticks to make 1 GB, you must make sure that they are both the same type and from the same manufacturer. RAM is notoriously finicky and doesn't play well with other modules, so even if you got two sticks that had the same speed rating they may not work properly if they were made by different companies. The safest bet is to buy a matched-pair set, which guarantees you compatibility.

5

Jargon buster

POST – Power On Self-Test, the check that every computer runs when it first powers up, to ensure that all necessary hardware is present and correct.

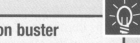

Installing a new hard disk

Unlike memory and graphics cards, there's a little more to fitting a hard disk. Although physically installing it is usually very easy, as simple to do as a new DVD drive, you must then format and configure the hard disk so that it's ready for use. If you're fitting it as a secondary drive, this is simpler as it will just need formatting. If you're going to be installing Windows and you're using a serial ATA hard disk, however, things get a little more complex. You will need to use a floppy disk containing the drivers for the HDD (hard disk drive) so Windows can recognise it.

Remove the old drive

1. Pop open your PC case and locate the drive bays holding the hard disk(s). Obviously, if you want to keep your current drive, you can skip this task entirely.

2. Unplug the power and data cables. These can be quite stiff so gently wiggle them from side to side until they loosen.

3. It used to be that all hard disks and other components were secured with screws – nowadays there's a good chance you have some kind of tool-less system, which makes life a great deal easier as the drives will usually just slide in and out. If they're screwed in, remove the screws and gently slide the drive from its bay. You may need to remove both side panels from your PC to get to screws on the other side.

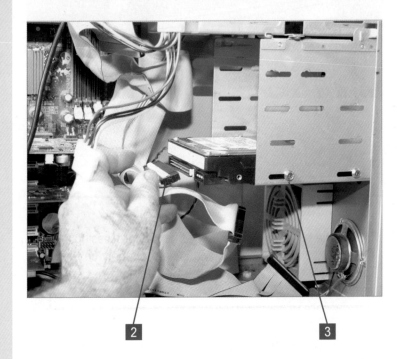

For your information

With the advent of serial ATA (SATA) drives, we no longer need to worry about master and slave configurations. SATA drives are hooked up to individual numbered connections on the board and do not share cables. Drive 0 is the first, 1 the second and so on.

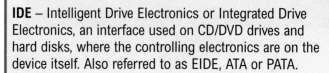

Installing a new hard disk (cont.)

Change the jumper settings

1. If you're fitting an IDE hard disk (the type with big fat ribbon cables) then you'll probably need to change the jumper settings. These tell the system what role the drive plays, whether it is the primary drive (master) or secondary (slave). SATA drive users can skip this entirely.

2. Look on the end of your hard disk – next to the power and data cable connections will be a small row of pins with a tiny piece of plastic covering two of them. This is the jumper.

3. On top of the drive will be a label showing the jumper setting. Pull the jumper plug out with tweezers (or long nails) and move it so that it covers the pins specified by the label for the setting you require. Master is usually the default.

5

Jargon buster

IDE – Intelligent Drive Electronics or Integrated Drive Electronics, an interface used on CD/DVD drives and hard disks, where the controlling electronics are on the device itself. Also referred to as EIDE, ATA or PATA.

Jumpers – a circuit bridge that allows the user to adjust the settings of a device by covering the jumper pins with a plastic plug.

SATA – Serial Advanced Technology Attachment, introduced to replace the ageing IDE interface. In addition to offering significant speed increases over IDE, SATA uses smaller cables, which helps with cable management and airflow inside the case.

Installing a new hard disk (cont.)

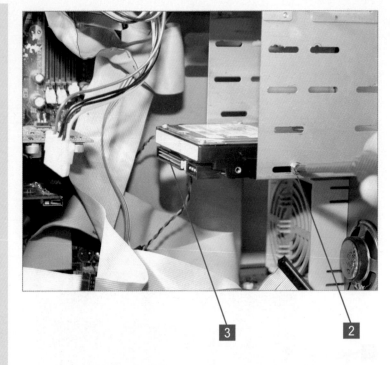

Fit the new hard disk

1 Take your new hard disk and slot it into a space in the drive bay. If you have a tool-less system you may need to clip on a bracket first so that it rides along the rails and clicks into place.

2 If your drives need to be screwed in, hold them in place and attach screws to either side of the drive bay. You can do it on one side only but it's less secure and may vibrate slightly, causing an irritating buzzing noise.

3 Hook up the power and data cables. If the drive is a replacement you can use the same cable that was attached to your old drive, otherwise you'll need to plug a new cable into your motherboard.

4 Seal up your PC and switch it on!

Important

!

If you're attaching a secondary IDE drive, it will need to be set as master or slave depending on where it's going. If you put it on the same cable as your current primary drive or a CD/DVD drive, set it as slave. If it's going on its own on the secondary IDE connection, use the master jumper setting.

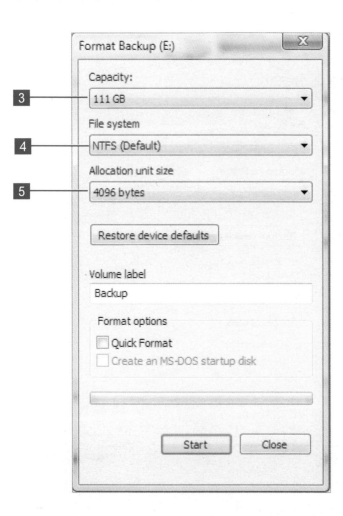

Set up your new drive

1 When you boot your system, you should see the extra drive listed during the POST. After this, one of two things will happen. Either your system will boot as normal or it will complain that no operating system has been found. If you're installing a fresh drive, dig out those rescue or Windows disks and install the operating system.

2 Assuming that you're just fitting a secondary drive, you'll want to get into Windows and format it. Open up My Computer and see if the drive is listed, if so, right-click and choose Format.

3 Capacity tells you the storage space of your hard disk.

4 Select a file system. Our only option here is NTFS, which is preferable anyway.

5 Leave the allocation size at the default setting.

Jargon buster

NTFS – NT File System, used by Windows NT and later versions of Windows, NTFS offers several advantages over FAT32 such as greater reliability and file and folder security.

Installing a new hard disk (cont.)

Set up your new drive (cont.)

6 Type a name for your drive in the volume label box, this is optional.

7 Quick Format will just do a quick sweep of the drive, use it if you just want to quickly clear one of your drives.

8 Click Start to begin formatting. The time this takes will vary depending on the size of the drive.

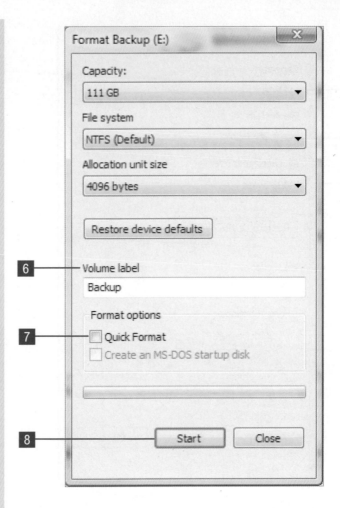

2

3

Using Disk Management

1 In the last steps we showed you how to set up a drive in Windows, but what if your hard disk isn't even showing in My Computer when you restart? This is easily fixed with Disk Management.

2 To bring up Disk Management, either right-click on My Computer and select Manage, or go to Start, Run and type compmgmt.msc then hit OK. Click Disk Management from the menu tree.

3 If your new drive appears with a black bar and says 'Unallocated', like our example, it means that it needs to be partitioned and formatted before use. Right-click and choose New Simple Volume.

4 Follow the New Volume wizard. Leave the default options as they are and don't change them unless you have a specific reason.

5

Timesaver tip

When you plug in a new external drive you may also find that is not listed either. If that happens, follow the steps for enabling and formatting a new hard disk.

Changing drive settings

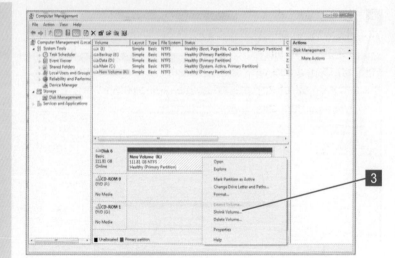

1 Now that your drive is partitioned and formatted, right-click on a disk in Disk Management to bring up a list of options. You can change the drive letter and related file paths, but be aware that this may result in some programs not working if they're unable to find files.

2 Clicking Format brings up the same drive formatting options as we looked at previously.

3 Shrink Volume allows you to change the size of the drive, freeing up additional space for a new partition.

Partitioning your disk – dividing the file space into multiple virtual drives – can help keep your data organised and also offers a quick 'n' dirty backup solution. Split a disk in two and you can format and wipe the other while safely storing data on the second half of it. Partitions are easily created using the Disk Management tool.

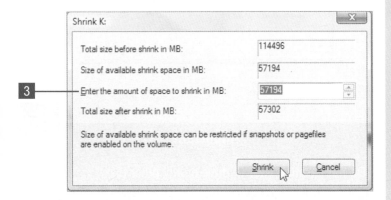

1 Back up all the data you want to keep and then right-click on the drive in Disk Management. You have two options – if the drive is new, you can format and select a file size that's smaller than its full capacity, leaving the remaining drive space for the new partition, or use the Shrink command to change the drive size without formatting.

2 For this example we'll use Shrink, so right-click and choose Shrink Volume.

3 By default, Windows will split the drive in half, but if you'd rather have one partition bigger than the other just adjust the amount of available drive space. Click Shrink to complete the process.

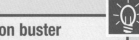

Jargon buster

Partition – to divide a hard disk into several individual parts. The operating system then sees each drive partition as a separate disk, as if you had multiple physical hard disks installed

5

Creating multiple partitions (cont.)

4 In Disk Management you'll see that your drive is now split into two.

5 Format the new partition by right-clicking and choosing the New Simple Volume command.

6 You can rejoin the two partitions by deleting one volume, then use the Extend Volume option on the remaining partition. With two partitions you must rejoin the full drive capacity, but Windows will assign the disk space itself.

Important

Do not partition your C: drive or any other disk containing an operating system, as it will wipe the data it contains. If you need to partition a hard disk that's in use you'll need to use a specialised tool like Norton PartitionMagic. It's recommended that you use this tool if you regularly partition your hard drives as it makes the process much easier and safer.

If you don't already have a DVD writer of some description, there's little excuse now that prices are so low. Good quality, brand name burners can be found for less than £30, and as well as allowing you to easily back up your system they'll also let you create your own DVD video disks. Installing a new optical drive is a similar procedure to fitting a hard disk, but with a lot less messing about afterwards, since there's no need to format or partition a DVD drive. Most drives, even now, are IDE although models using the SATA interface are slowly coming on sale. Like hard disks IDE optical drives must be configured for master or slave, they can also share a cable with a hard disk.

2

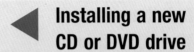

Installing a new CD or DVD drive

Remove the current drive

1 Pull out the power and data cables from the drive.

2 Locate the screws or mechanism holding the drive in place and remove them.

3 Slide the drive out from the front of your case.

5

Installing a new CD or DVD drive (cont.)

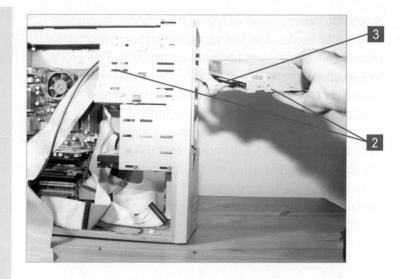

Install the new drive

1. Slide the drive into the gap from the front of the case. If you're adding a second drive, you'll need to pop out a faceplate and possibly twist off the metal plate behind that. Don't forget to set the master/slave configuration in the same way as a hard disk.

2. Line up the holes on the side of the drive with those on the drive cage and screw the drive down. As with a hard disk, it's a good idea to do this on both sides of the cage, especially since optical drives can make a real racket as they spin.

3. Connect up the power and data cables.

4. Optical drives also have CD-audio outputs, if you have a cable for this going into your soundcard or onboard sound then you should also plug in the 'CD-OUT' connector.

5. Once the drive is connected, start your system. It will automatically be detected and no software is needed. You may, however, need to reinstall any disk-burning software so it can detect the new drive.

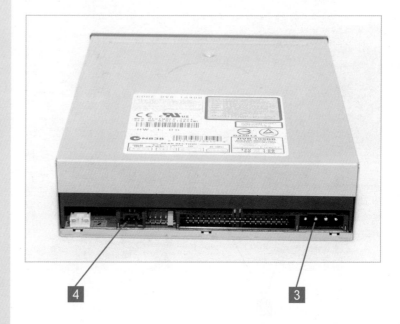

Device Manager is the central point in Windows for monitoring your hardware. It contains the details of every component and attached peripheral, with options for managing each one. If you encounter problems with an item of hardware, you can use the Device Manager to uninstall and reinstall the device, roll back the driver to a previous version.

Managing your hardware with Device Manager

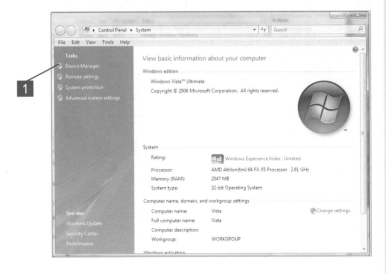

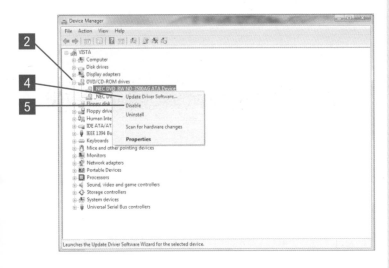

Use Device Manager

1 Go to Control Panel. If you're using the Classic View, double-click System and choose Device Manager from the tasks list. If you're using the Control Panel Home interface, go to Hardware & Sound then click Device Manager.

2 Click the + button next to each item in the tree to expand the view and see further details on the hardware.

3 Right-click on an item of hardware to view the available options.

4 Click Update Driver to have Windows search for a newer version of the driver software. It's generally better to find newer drivers for yourself, though.

5 Click Disable to switch off the device. It will stay off until activated again and will not be detected by Windows when you restart.

5

Managing your hardware with Device Manager (cont.)

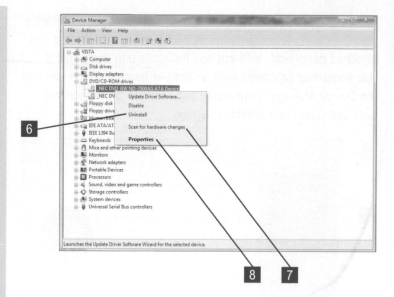

6 Click Uninstall to completely remove the hardware from Windows. If you reboot and the hardware is still present in your computer, Windows will detect it and attempt to set it up again.

7 Scan for hardware changes can be used to find hardware after you've uninstalled it.

8 Click Properties to bring up more information about the selected hardware device.

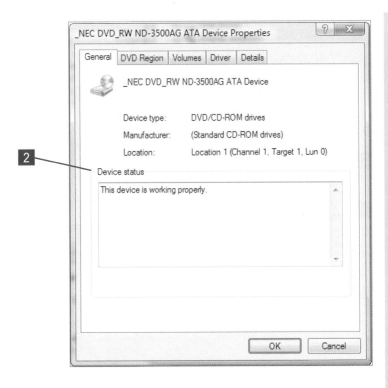

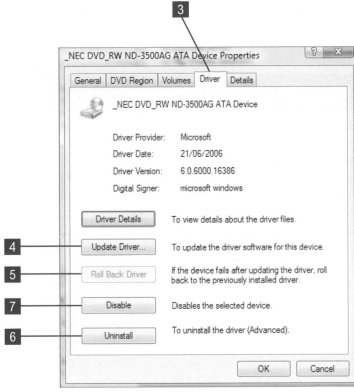

Managing your hardware with Device Manager (cont.)

Learn about hardware properties

1 The Properties window of each device varies wildly, with some having several options and others with little to no information.

2 In the General tab you'll find information about the current status of the device.

3 The Driver tab is available in the Properties for much of the hardware and gives you information about the currently installed driver software.

4 Click Update Driver to search online for a newer version.

5 Roll Back Driver will restore your system to use the previously installed driver.

6 Uninstall will remove the driver and require re-installation of the hardware device.

7 You can stop the hardware from working on your system by clicking Disable. This is not a permanent change, but it will not be available to use until you re-enable it.

Managing your hardware with Device Manager (cont.)

1 One unique option of DVD drives is the ability to select another region. Click the Region tab, choose a country from the list and click OK to set that region.

2 The Changes remaining number tells you how many times you're allowed to set the region before it's locked.

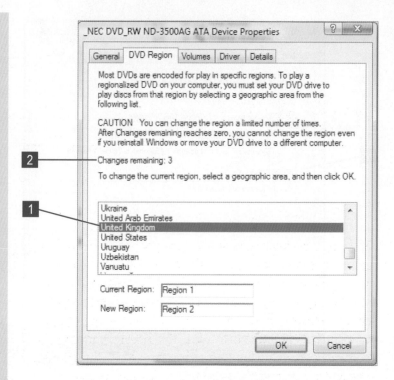

_NEC DVD_RW ND-3500AG ATA Device Properties

General | DVD Region | Volumes | Driver | Details

Most DVDs are encoded for play in specific regions. To play a regionalized DVD on your computer, you must set your DVD drive to play discs from that region by selecting a geographic area from the following list.

CAUTION You can change the region a limited number of times. After Changes remaining reaches zero, you cannot change the region even if you reinstall Windows or move your DVD drive to a different computer.

2 — Changes remaining: 3

To change the current region, select a geographic area, and then click OK.

1 —
Ukraine
United Arab Emirates
United Kingdom
United States
Uruguay
Uzbekistan
Vanuatu

Current Region: Region 1

New Region: Region 2

OK   Cancel

For your information

Devices that are not functioning correctly will be flagged with warning icons and their menu view already expanded when you open Device Manager. This will include hardware that is disabled or not installed. You can then right-click it as normal and take the appropriate action to resolve the problem.

Internet

Introduction

Like or not, the Internet is now an integral part of the modern computing experience, you're missing out on half the fun if you've got a PC and you're not online. Assuming you've got antivirus and a firewall (see Chapter 3 for more information) getting on the net is easy and safe. If you just want to send some email and browse the web, a 56k dial-up connection is the cheapest method, but to get the most out of it you'll want to be looking at an ADSL or cable broadband connection. There are hundreds of different services offering speeds from 256k right up to 10 MB and beyond, with prices that vary from as little as £9.99 per month. Two things to watch out for though are contract length and bandwidth limits. Some companies will give you a monthly contract, so you can cancel without any penalty, while annual contracts will incur a charge if you cancel. Bandwidth limits are imposed to stop heavy users taking all the resources. You will be given an allowance, in GB transferred per month. Going over that will either result in your speed being reduced or a charge for the additional data. If you're planning on heavy use, get a service without any limit. We're going to look at web browsing, email and instant messaging in this chapter. Apart from Messenger, we've ignored the usual Microsoft products, simply because their popularity and insecurity can be a danger to new users. Alternatives such as Firefox have more features and better security than the ubiquitous Internet Explorer.

What you'll do

Install the web browser Firefox

Configure Firefox

Use Firefox Add-ons

Browse the web with Firefox

Manage bookmarks

Set up an email account

Use Fastmail

Send email

Configure Fastmail

Make the most of Fastmail's features

Configure Live Messenger

Manage Contacts

Chat with Messenger

Send and receive files

Jargon buster

Bandwidth – the amount of data that can be transmitted within a certain amount of time. For Internet connections, this is bps, bytes per second.

Email – electronic mail, messages sent over an electronic network, stored in a server until the recipient reads them.

Instant Messaging – a method of communication that creates a private chat room between yourself and at least one other person. Instant Messaging can be used to send text or files.

Since 1999, Internet Explorer has been the dominant web browser with over 90% of the market share. However, the past few years have seen a backlash against Internet Explorer fuelled by countless security holes that left PCs wide open to attack from viruses, spyware and malicious websites. Mozilla, the open-source offshoot of Netscape, has taken advantage of the situation, first releasing the fully-featured Mozilla web browser and, more recently, its slimmed-down sibling Firefox. The latter has become hugely popular thanks to its security, speed and customisation options, which is why we're using it here. This totally free application is not only safer but also makes browsing the web a smoother, more enjoyable experience.

Installing the web browser Firefox

6

1 Pop over to www.firefox.com and enter the website.

2 Click the Download link and save the installation file to your hard disk.

3 Double-click the Firefox installation file.

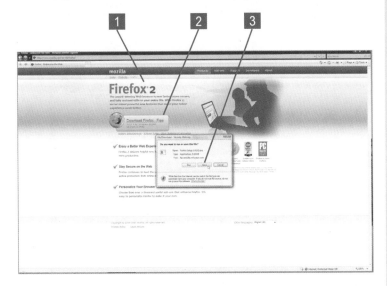

For your information

As well as Internet Explorer and Firefox, there are many other alternative web browsers for you to choose. Netscape (www.netscape.com) is still around, but is a modified version of the Gecko engine that Firefox is built upon. The next most popular browser after Internet Explorer and Firefox is Opera (www.opera.com), which offers similar compatibility to Firefox but boasts an extensive range of features. There's also a slew of browsers based upon Internet Explorer, some free and some shareware, which add features like tabbed browsing and pop-up blocking to the world's number one browser.

Installing the web browser Firefox (cont.)

4 Click through the license agreement and select Standard or Custom installation. We'll go with Custom, but Standard just uses the default installation options.

5 Choose whether you want to install the Developer Tools and Quality Feedback Agent. Unless you're a web developer the tools will be useless, but Quality Feedback Agent allows you to send in bug reports when Firefox crashes, which can assist the development team.

6 Check or uncheck the boxes to choose where shortcut icons will be placed.

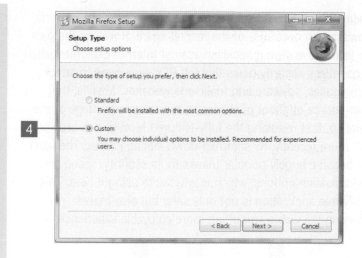

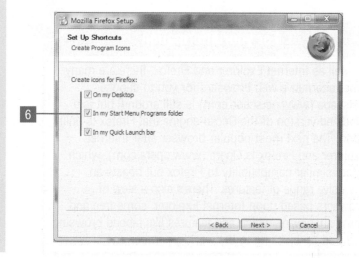

Firefox is packed with options that allow you to customise its behaviour to suit your needs. It's also got a great range of security features that help protect your privacy and make logging on to your secure, password-protected websites easier. After installing Firefox you should always take a few minutes to familiarise yourself with its options and features.

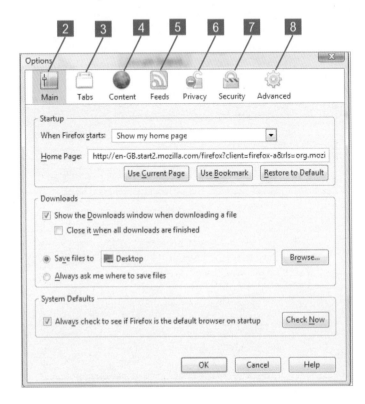

Configuring Firefox

6

Change Firefox settings

1 Open the Tools menu on the toolbar and click Options.

2 The Main tab contains miscellaneous options for the browser.

3 The Tabs options allow you to adjust how new windows and tabs are handled, so you can open all new windows in tabs, for example.

4 Content includes options for handling external scripts and pop-up windows as well as colours and fonts.

5 Configure RSS news feeds and Firefox's Live Bookmarks feature.

6 The privacy options let you configure browser history and manage cookies.

7 Use the options in Security to protect yourself when browsing the web.

8 More controls for Firefox, including connection and update settings.

Jargon buster

FTP – File Transfer Protocol, a method for downloading and uploading files to another system over a network. If you're creating a webpage you will usually have to login via FTP to upload the files.

Proxy server – sits between your computer and the server you're trying to access, so the proxy receives the data and sends it on to you. Proxies are often used as a method of anonymously browsing the Internet, since the rest of the Net sees the proxy details and not yours.

Configuring
Firefox (cont.)

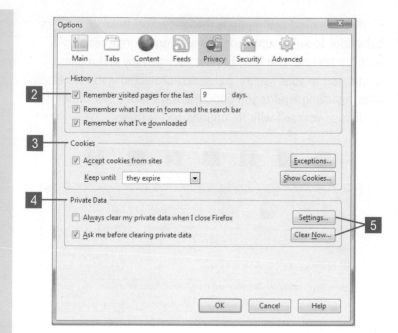

Change privacy and security settings

1 Use the Privacy tab to manage stored passwords, cookies and other data.

2 You can choose how long Firefox will remember the sites visited by entering a number in the box. It can also keep a record of files downloaded and information entered in forms and searches. This is useful as it saves time when registering for sites and so on, but if you're on a shared system it's best to disable all these settings.

3 Cookies also allow you to use the special features of websites and some will not work at all without them. This means that if you do disable cookies you will have to use the Exception option occasionally to grant access to specific pages.

4 For extra security you can have Firefox delete information like sites visited and stored form data by enabling this option.

Options

Main   Tabs   Content   Feeds   Privacy   Security   Advanced

7 ☑ Warn me when sites try to install add-ons   Exceptions...

8 ☑ Tell me if the site I'm visiting is a suspected forgery
    ◉ Check using a downloaded list of suspected sites
    ○ Check by asking   Google ▼   about each site I visit

Passwords
☑ Remember passwords for sites   Exceptions...
☐ Use a master password   Change Master Password...
    Show Passwords...

Warning Messages
Choose which warning messages you want to see while browsing the web   Settings...

OK   Cancel   Help

5 If you choose to have Firefox wipe privacy data, click Settings to configure exactly what will be deleted. You can also clear privacy data straight away with the Clear Now button.

6 Further options for protecting your privacy are found in the Security tab.

7 Some websites will attempt to install additional software in your browser. This represents a security risk so by default Firefox will warn you whenever it happens and give you the option to add the site to the exception list so it will be allowed without prompting the next time you visit.

8 A useful new feature is phishing protection which checks the authenticity of sites you visit, either by using a master list of suspect sites or a search on Google. This protects you from being fooled into visiting fake banking or shopping sites.

Jargon buster

Pop-up – a window that pops up uninvited, usually for advertising. They can be very irratating and without a blocker your system can be flooded. There are also pop-unders, which appear underneath your browser.

Configuring Firefox (cont.)

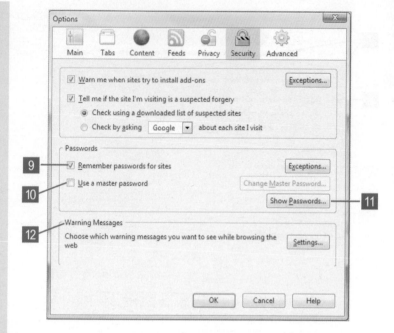

9 The Saved Passwords options allow you to control website passwords you've saved. You can stop Firefox from saving passwords by clearing the Remember passwords box.

10 Click Use a master password to protect your saved password data.

11 Show Passwords will show you the saved usernames and passwords.

12 Enable or disable certain warning messages. It's best to leave these as they are unless you know what you're doing, as they can give you an early warning of insecure websites.

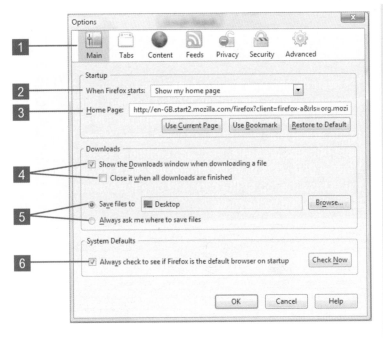

Download options

1 In the Main tab you'll find options relating to downloads and the home page settings.

2 Select what you would like Firefox to display each time you open a new browser window. This can be your home page, a blank page or it can restore the windows and tabs from your last session.

3 You can change the default home page, which is what appears when each browser opens and when you click the home button on the browser toolbar.

4 Change the behaviour of the download manager. If you uncheck Show Download Manager you'll never see it except for a notification when files are done.

5 Select where you want downloaded files saved, choose Ask Me to have Firefox prompt you each time or set a default location by clicking Browse.

6 Click the Default Browser box and Firefox will check to see if it's still the default browser. If not, it will ask if you want to change or keep the current browser.

Timesaver tip

Anytime you're in the browser, press Ctrl+J to bring up the Firefox Download Manager. Also, if you've chosen a default save location, you can save any file to an alternative directory by right-clicking and choosing Save As.

Configuring Firefox (cont.)

Content options

1. Disable the block pop-up option to stop Firefox from suppressing pop-up windows.

2. Uncheck Load images to switch off images in Firefox.

3. Adding sites by clicking Exceptions next to each option allows you to automatically load images, JavaScript and pop-ups when these options are disabled, and also block them from specific sites when you have them enabled.

4. Disabling Java and Javascript will stop websites that use these features from working. Javascript in particular can be a security vulnerability so you may want to keep it switched off until needed.

5. The Advanced options tell Firefox what Javascript applications are allowed to do, this includes resizing and moving windows.

6. When certain files are recognised by Firefox you can change their behaviour by clicking the Manage button and choosing an alternative program association. This will only affect Firefox and not the rest of Windows.

176

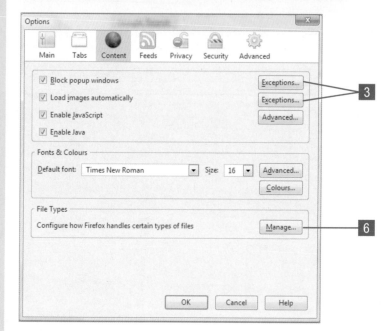

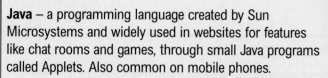

Jargon buster

Java – a programming language created by Sun Microsystems and widely used in websites for features like chat rooms and games, through small Java programs called Applets. Also common on mobile phones.

Javascript – not related to Java, a scripting language created by Netscape for the production of interactive websites. It is supported by most modern web browsers.

5 **3** **2** **4** **1**

Options

Main   Tabs   Content   Feeds   Privacy   Security   Advanced

General | Network | Update | Encryption

Automatically check for updates to:

- ☑ Firefox
- ☑ Installed Add-ons
- ☑ Search Engines

When updates to Firefox are found:

- ○ Ask me what I want to do
- ⦿ Automatically download and install the update
  - ☑ Warn me if this will disable any of my add-ons

Show Update History

OK   Cancel   Help

Use advanced options

1 The Advanced tab contains a selection of miscellaneous settings, including options for SSL security, site validation and updates.

2 Firefox can automatically download new updates to your Add-ons, search engines and the browser itself. Click the Update tab to configure this feature.

3 The Network tab contains options for changing your connection settings. If you are on a network you can manually enter an IP address and other details and also configure a proxy server if you have one, which can be used for anonymous web browsing.

4 The Encryption tab includes options for SSL and site certificates, used for accessing secure websites. It's best to leave these at the default settings.

5 Within General you'll find some accessibility options to help make navigating sites easier, and some miscellaneous settings for spell checking and page scrolling.

Using Firefox Add-ons

Among Firefox's many features, Add-ons are considered to be one of the 'killer apps'. Tiny, free software modules created by Firefox users that extend the browser's capabilities, hundreds of Add-ons can be downloaded from the Firefox website and whether you think you need them or not it's almost guaranteed that something will catch your eye. Thanks to the way Firefox has been designed, installing and managing Add-ons is dead easy.

Download and install Add-ons

1. First off, head to the Add-ons site at http://addons.mozilla.org.

2. Noteworthy Add-ons are highlighted on the main site.

3. Begin browsing the available Add-ons by clicking the Extensions link to the left.

4. Enter a term in the search box to find Add-ons.

5. Click an Add-on and you'll be taken to its download page. Read the information here to check the Add-on features and requirements.

6. Check that the Add-on supports your version of Firefox. This Add-on works with everything from Firefox 0.8 upwards.

7. Read the user comments to find out if there are any problems, or just to see what other users thought about the Add-on.

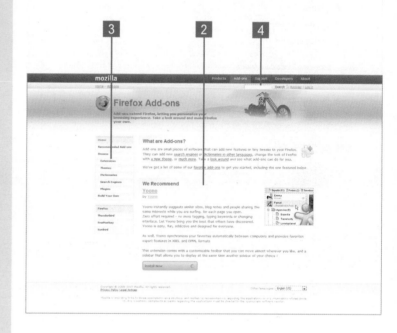

For your information

One of the most useful Add-ons is BugMeNot (www.bugmenot.com), which stores logins for hundreds of sites. The purpose of this is to save you signing up for a free registration every single time you want to view a news article or access any other content. It's a real time-saver and a definite must-have for eager web surfers.

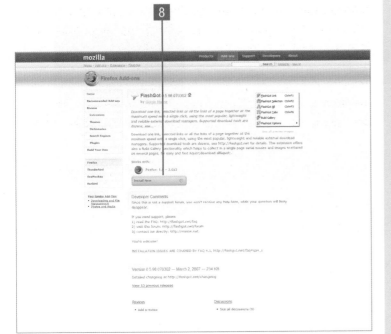

8 When you click Install you may see a warning bar appear at the top of the screen. If this happens, click Options then add the site to the Allow list so you can continue the installation.

9 The Software Installation dialogue will pop up, listing the Add-on you've chosen. Click Install Now.

Installation only takes a second in most cases and once it's done the Add-on window will appear. Usually you will need to restart Firefox.

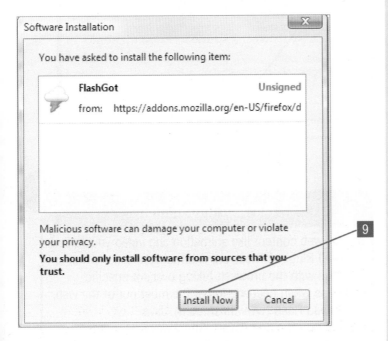

Using Firefox
Add-ons (cont.)

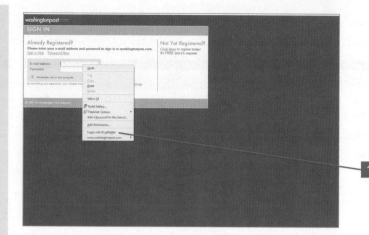

Use Add-ons

1. Most Add-ons are used either by right-clicking within Firefox or from a toolbar button. The two Add-ons installed in our example, BugMeNot and FlashGot, are both on the right-click menu.

2. For BugMeNot, we simply right-click on a web form and choose the BugMeNot option. Some Add-ons will open windows or display further options.

3. From the Firefox toolbar, click Tools and select Add-ons. Here you can view and manage your installed Add-ons.

4. Click Uninstall to remove the selected Add-on.

5. Update will check for newer versions.

6. Options displays settings specific to each Add-on.

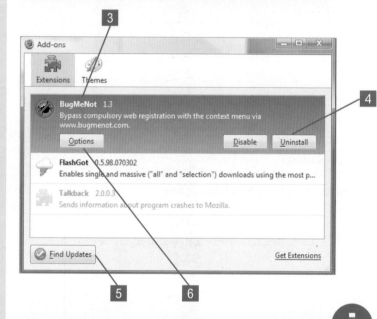

For your information

To play web content like animation and video you'll need to install Plugins. These are external applications that interface with the browser, taking over for specific functions when needed. To get the most out of the web, you'll need Flash (www.flash.com), Java (http://www.sun.com/java/), Shockwave (www.shockwave.com), Real Player (www.real.com), QuickTime (www.apple.com/quicktime) and the latest version of Media Player (www.microsoft.com).

Type in the web address and hit Enter – that's pretty much it! Browsing websites is a very painless experience, especially when using Firefox. And despite what the tabloids may say, provided you've got your security suitably beefed up (see Chapter 3) you don't need to worry about viruses, hackers or other unpleasantness. You'll quickly discover the simple joys of tabbed browsing, too, especially if you've only ever used Internet Explorer before.

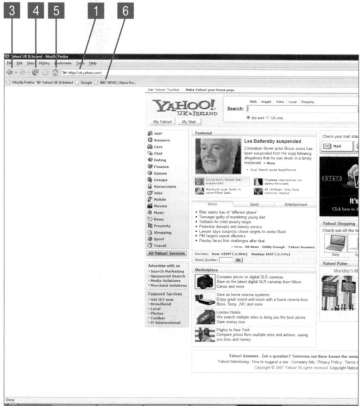

View and navigate websites

1 Type a web address into the address bar and hit Enter or click the Go button to visit the site, it will be displayed in the main browser window. Click the arrow on the address bar to see previously visited sites.

2 Firefox includes a built-in Search. Type a search term into the box and hit Enter.

3 Use the Back and Forward buttons to move between sites previously viewed in your current session.

4 Click Reload to refresh the current web page.

5 Click the Home button to go back to your defined home page. Set this in the Options menu.

6 The Bookmark toolbar can store your favourite web pages for quick access.

Timesaver tip

If you type the name of a website into the address bar without putting www. or a domain name, Firefox will run a search and take you to the first matching site. This is useful if you're visiting a popular site like Amazon or IMDB, as you can go there quickly without having to type the full address.

Browsing the web with Firefox (cont.)

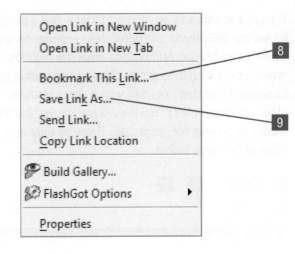

Open Link in New Window
Open Link in New Tab

Bookmark This Link...
Save Link As...
Send Link...
Copy Link Location

Build Gallery...
FlashGot Options ▶

Properties

7 Right-click on a link or image to bring up further options. The tabbed browsing feature allows you to open links in new tabs as well as new windows, which is very useful for reducing desktop clutter.

8 Click Bookmark this Link to save the link and add it to your favourites.

9 Save Link As will allow you to save the linked file to a location on your hard disk. You can also copy the link or send it via email.

Timesaver tip

Open a new tab quickly in Firefox by hitting Ctrl+T. Open a link in a new tab by holding Ctrl when you click.

Jargon buster

HTTP – HyperText Transfer Protocol, the system used to display web pages, this tells a server that you're visiting to view a website. Sites beginning with www do not have to be prefixed with HTTP but those without, for example images.google.com, must have http:// placed in front.

Plugins – additional software applications that are called by a web browser when needed to perform a specific function. Common plugins include Flash, QuickTime and Shockwave.

If you've not already, you'll soon realise how important and useful the Bookmark function is when browsing the web. With the number of sites out there you need something to help you keep track, and Firefox offers plenty of options for storing your favourite sites. You can bookmark a page just like normal, but also place your very favourite sites in the Bookmark toolbar to make them instantly accessible. There's even a user-friendly Bookmark Manager to help you keep all those links organised.

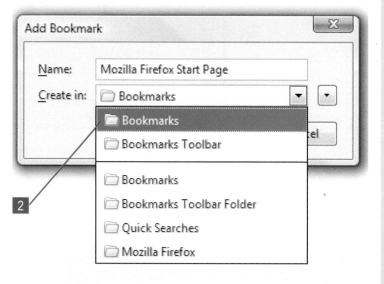

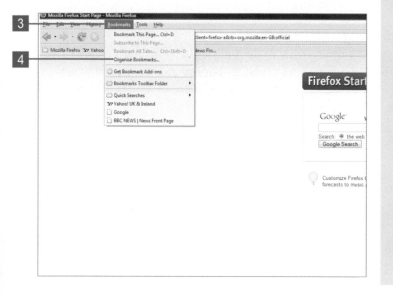

Bookmark a site

1 Want to save a link to that site? Hit Ctrl+D or right-click on the page.

2 A dialogue box will appear asking where you want to save the link. Click the drop-down menu and choose Bookmarks, Bookmarks Toolbar or one of the recently used folders.

3 Click Bookmarks from the toolbar and you can view any bookmarks you've saved.

4 Click Organise Bookmarks to bring up the Bookmarks Manager.

Managing bookmarks (cont.)

Edit your bookmarks

1. Your bookmark folders appear down the side.

2. Drag links into the Bookmarks Toolbar Folder to add them to your Bookmarks toolbar. They will appear in the main Firefox window.

3. Select a folder and right-click to bring up various options.

4. You can add a new bookmark, create a new bookmark folder or add a separator to organise your bookmarks.

5. Click the Properties option from the Context menu or toolbar to see more information about a folder or link and edit the data.

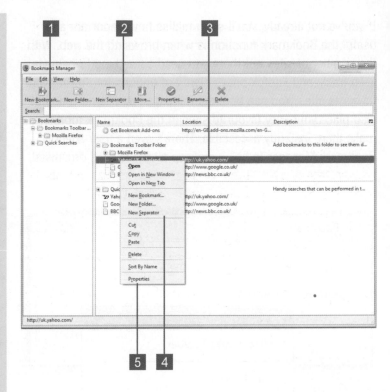

Important

If you've got important links stored you should regularly back them up. Click File in the Bookmarks Manager and select Export. You can then save your Bookmarks file to a location on your hard disk. If you need to restore the bookmarks, select the Import option.

Aside from browsing the web, you'll spend a large amount of your time online sending and receiving email. You'll get a basic email service from your Internet service provider (ISP) but most choose to go with an alternative free or paid-for service offering more features. By far the most popular is Microsoft's Hotmail, but its popularity has meant that good, memorable addresses are increasingly scarce and any account opened gets almost immediately flooded by spam. Thankfully there's no shortage of alternatives. We've chosen Fastmail, a fantastic email provider that provides a basic, but still useful, free service and some reasonably priced premium accounts.

Setting up an email account

6

1 Type www.fastmail.co.uk into your web browser and on the front page, click the Sign Up Now link for one of the account types.

2 You'll now need to choose an email address. For free accounts this must be at least seven characters. You can click the drop-down menu to select an alternative domain name.

3 Type a password for your account. Repeat it to confirm you've typed it correctly.

4 Enter your name.

5 You will need to enter another email address so the details of your new account can be confirmed. It's also used to retrieve your account details in case you forget.

6 If another Fastmail user referred you, enter their username here.

7 Read the terms of service and click Agree (if you agree) and then Signup.

8 Read the confirmation mail that is sent to your alternative address and click the link to activate your account.

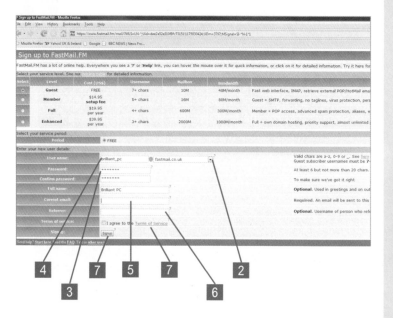

Setting up an email account (cont.)

Jargon buster

Spam – junk email, named after the food product or the famous Monty Python sketch, depending on who you ask. Spam has become a huge problem with billions of mails sent every year hawking anything from Viagra to dubious loan offers. Most, if not all, email providers should now have some level of spam filtering.

Important

Fastmail checks the password you enter when signing up – if it sees a dictionary word you'll be asked to confirm that you want to have it, as such words are very easy to crack. For the best security you should use a mix of numbers and letters.

Compared to the fairly simplistic interface of Hotmail, Fastmail can appear quite confusing at first. This is only because it packs so many features however and once you've got used to the large number of options it's as easy to use as any other webmail service. Of course, once you do understand all the functions available you'll find it a far more flexible service than most other email providers.

Use the Fastmail interface

1 Your inbox and other folders are listed down the left-hand side.

2 The Resource Usage meters show how much of your storage space and bandwidth have been used. Paid accounts include larger bandwidth limits.

3 Use the drop-down Action menu, check the box next to the message(s) you want to perform the action on, then click the Do button.

4 Email is displayed here. Click the From address to send a mail, or the Subject to read the message.

5 Search your messages.

Timesaver tip

Don't have an alternative email address? There's a site that can help you – www.mailinator.com. You can send mail to anything @mailinator.com and it creates a temporary inbox. Go to the site, type in the address you used and your mail will be waiting. This is great for avoiding spam when you want to sign up for message boards, or if you need to use a service like Fastmail and you don't already have an address. Remember though, the alternative address in Fastmail is used to retrieve your login details when you've forgotten them and since Mailinator doesn't use any passwords, you should change it as soon as possible.

Sending an email

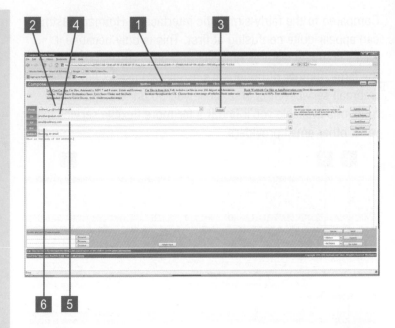

1 Click Compose.

2 In the From box, you can select an alternative address to send mail from by clicking the arrow to display other personalities.

3 Click the Change button to enter a custom From address.

4 In the To field, type in the address to which you're sending email; separate addresses with a comma to send to multiple recipients.

5 Use the Cc field to send a copy of the mail to another address.

6 Bcc will send a copy to the specified addresses without revealing the recipients' details to other people receiving the message.

Important

Be careful when attaching files to your email. Not only does the free Fastmail service have a limited bandwidth allowance for sending and receiving mail, but most servers will reject large attachments. Try not to send anything larger than about 1 MB unless you know the person receiving it can accept the file.

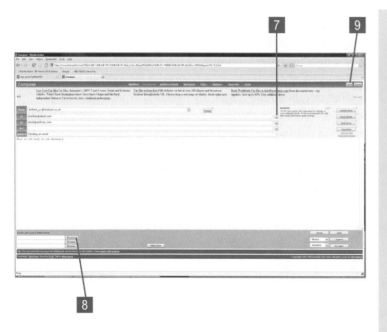

7 Click Address Book to add stored names to the To, Cc and Bcc fields.

8 To attach a file to your message, click Browse and select it from your disks.

9 When you're done entering the details for your email, click Send. To save it for later, click Save Draft.

Once you've sent an email, you'll be shown a confirmation and asked if you want to add unrecognised addresses to your Address Book.

Timesaver tip

If you're sending a mass email and don't want everyone to see the other email addresses, put all the recipients in the Bcc field and your own address in the To field.

Configuring Fastmail

Fastmail has an extensive range of options and features that allow you to customise the behaviour of the interface and the way it handles emails. As well as the standard array of user preferences, you can use an advanced rules system to protect against unwanted messages, by rejecting email based on specified criteria or shuttling it into a particular folder. It is easy to set up auto-respond and forwarding for your messages, but the rule options are deceptively simple. As you become more accustomed to its features it's possible to use complex commands and perform all manner of useful tricks. Although Fastmail's spam protection features work incredibly well, you can use the rules to define your own custom spam filters.

Change your account preferences

1. Click Options, then Preferences.

2. In the User/Account section, you can change the name that appears when you send email, change the backup email address and set your time zone.

3. In Display, you can match the Fastmail interface to your screen resolution and select an alternative style sheet.

4. Use the Compose options to change settings for sending email, such as auto-completing addresses and text entry mode.

5. Don't change the View settings unless you're sure about what you're doing. Not only do these options affect the character set for typing and reading mails, there are also some important settings that protect you from phishing and spam mails.

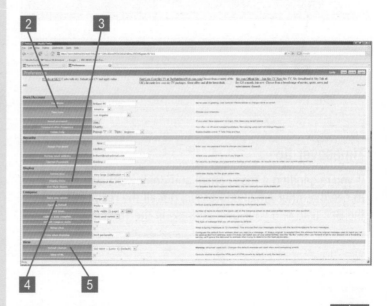

Jargon buster

Phishing – a con using fake email and websites that tricks victims into entering sensitive details for online banks and other services such as Paypal and Ebay. The emails often tell you that your account is going to expire and give a link to reactivate. Although the link looks genuine it is actually going to a totally different location set up by the scammers. Phishing mails can often be spotted by the abundance of spelling and grammar mistakes, but in any case banks and other sites will never ask you to enter your details via email.

Configuring Fastmail (cont.)

6

Create custom rules

1 From the Options screen, click Define Rules.

2 You can automatically reject emails that meet certain criteria. First select where Fastmail should check, by selecting from the 'Look In' category drop-down menu.

3 Enter the text you want it to search for in Text Matching.

4 Check the Silent box to reject emails without notifying the sender. Click Add to save the new rule.

5 Manage messages with large attachments by entering a maximum file size and choosing whether you want to reject them straight off or move to another folder.

6 Enter a secret word and give it to your friends. They can use that in the subject line and their messages will always bypass the filters you set up.

Timesaver tip

Block email from an entire domain by selecting the From option and just entering '@TheDomainYouWantToBlock.com' into the text matching field. This will reject all messages coming from any address at this domain and is useful for blocking persistent spammers. Don't do it unless you're sure you're not going to need email from there!

Configuring Fastmail (cont.)

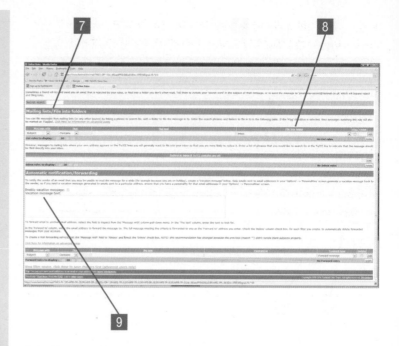

7 Automatically move messages matching criteria you choose into a specific folder using the Mailing Lists/File Into Folders filter.

8 As before, tell Fastmail where to look and enter some text for the filter, but you'll also need to choose which folder you want the messages moved into.

9 You can set an away auto-response by checking the Enable Vacation Message box and typing your message into the text box. This message will be automatically sent to anyone who emails you when it's active.

Among the many features Fastmail offers, two in particular stand out. Its Personalities function allows you to create new personalities for sending email, so you can make it look as though email is coming from another location and use an alternative address for receiving replies, helping to keep your messages organised. The other is the POP Links feature. Enter the login details for a POP3 or Hotmail account and Fastmail will check those accounts for new mail, delivering them to your Inbox (or any other folder.) Combined with the Personalities option, this allows you to manage separate email accounts under one interface.

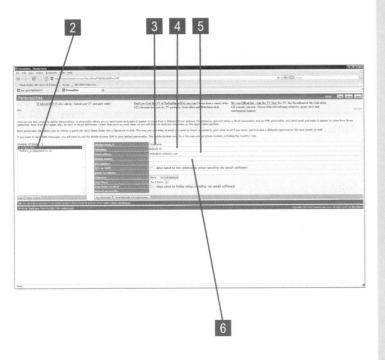

Create new Personalities

1 Go to Options and click the Personalities link.

2 Double-click on Create New to start entering the details for the personality.

3 Enter a display name – this will be what people receiving messages see.

4 Enter your full name.

5 Choose a From address. This can be anything, but when people reply they'll be replying to that address, so if it's fake you won't get any responses.

6 Optionally, you can enter your mobile number. Fastmail includes a text messaging feature which requires your mobile number to work.

Jargon buster

POP – Post Office Protocol, the most common email protocol. The latest version, POP3, can both send and receive email.

Making the most of Fastmail's features (cont.)

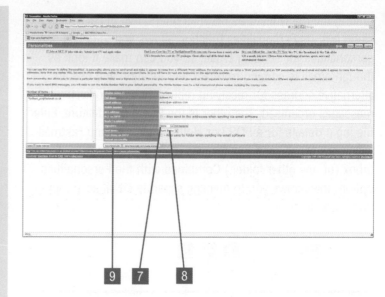

9   7   8

7 Select a signature. You can use the default or create one in the Signatures section of the Options menu.

8 Select the folder where copies of messages you've sent will be stored.

9 Click Save to store the Personality and Done to exit the section. It will now be available in the From menu when you compose a new message.

Timesaver tip

Personalities can be incredibly useful if you occasionally work from home or want to separate professional email from personal. Just set up a Personality with your work email as the From address, and when you email from home it'll look like you're slogging away in the office. Don't forget that replies will be sent to whatever email address you give.

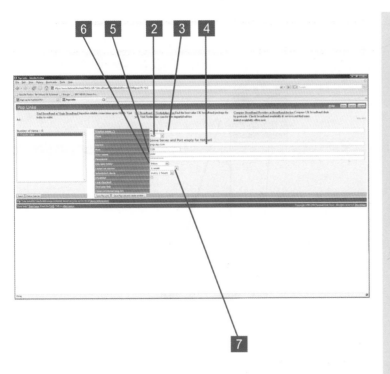

Retrieve Hotmail and ISP email through Fastmail

1 Go to Pop Links in the Options menu and start creating a new POP link.

2 Choose a display name for your POP mailbox. Make it memorable.

3 Select whether you want to retrieve mail from a POP or Hotmail account.

4 Enter the server and server port details. If you do not know these, contact your email provider. Leave blank if you chose Hotmail.

5 Type in the username and password you use to login to the account.

6 Choose the folder in which you want the retrieved messages to be placed.

7 Select how long messages will be kept on the original server. This can be up to 6 months and would allow you to download them again if you lose the copies.

Making the most of Fastmail's features (cont.)

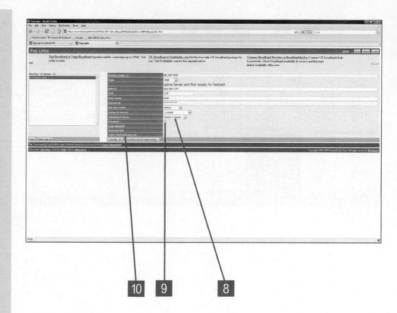

8 Choose whether to check for new mail manually or automatically, every few hours.

9 If Disabled is checked, it means Fastmail has failed to connect to the server five times in a row. Check that the details are correct then clear Disabled and save.

10 If you wish to download messages again, use the Clear Stored IDs option. If the originals are still on the POP server they will be retrieved the next time the account is checked.

Instant Messaging is a great way of keeping in contact with friends and relatives across the world. Once you have your friends on your contact list, you'll be able to see whenever they're online and chat to them in real-time. You can also send files and even use voice and video chat. There are many different Instant Messaging applications available, such as AOL Instant Messenger, ICQ, Skype and Yahoo! Messenger, but for this example we'll be using Microsoft's Live Messenger since it's the most popular Instant Messenger network and can be used instantly by anyone who has a Hotmail, Passport or Live ID account.

Download Messenger

1 Visit http://messenger.msn.com.

2 If you already have a Hotmail, Passport or Live ID account click the download link to get the latest version of Live Messenger.

3 If you do not have a valid account you'll need to click the Live ID link to sign up for a free account.

4 If you have an older version of Live or MSN Messenger, click this link to upgrade.

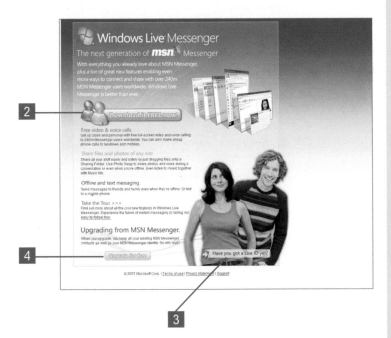

Configuring Live Messenger (cont.)

Use the MSN Interface

1 When Messenger is installed, its icon will be displayed in your system tray. Double-click this to bring up the login screen, enter the email address and password you chose for your account.

2 Check the Remember Me and/or Remember Password options to save you typing your details every time, or use the automatic sign-in to have Messenger log you in without any input.

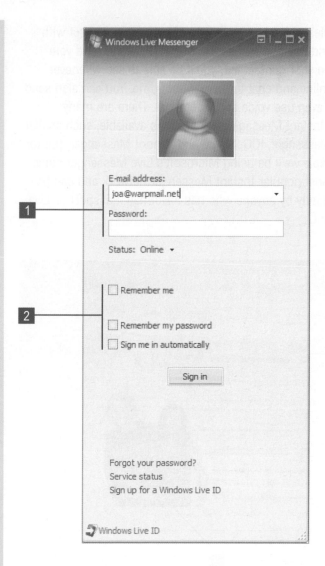

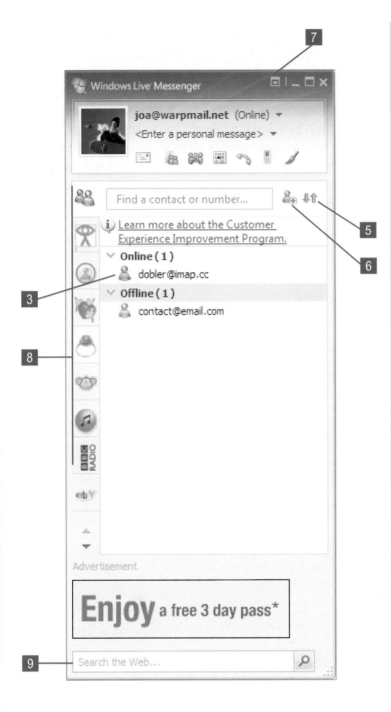

3 All your contacts are listed here in the main window. The current status of users will be shown along with other details.

4 Your details are shown at the top, with your name and picture.

5 This option allows you to sort your contacts using various criteria. For example, you can group people by their status, quickly showing you who is online and who is offline.

6 This is the Add Contacts button, click it to add your friends to your contact list.

7 It's not obvious, but this tiny button brings up the Messenger Options menu where you add contacts, edit preferences and access various other features.

8 These tabs allow you to switch between different services available through Messenger. For example, you can browse Ebay or receive help using Messenger.

9 Search the web via MSN Search by entering a term in the search field.

Managing Contacts

Messenger is useless without having your friends on it to chat, so the first thing you'll want to do is to add them to your contact list. You do this by inputting their email address – if they have not registered you can send them an email asking them to get online so you can chat. If they have registered, contacts will be asked if they want you to add them first, you will also see the same prompt when someone attempts to add you to their contact list. You may also want to delete contacts from your list, or you can block them so it looks as though you're always offline.

Add a contact

1 To add a new contact click the Add Contact button on the main Live Messenger interface.

2 Enter the email address of the person you want to add. You can also type in a greeting.

3 Your contact list is like an address book – these options let you store postal addresses and other details.

4 When you're ready, click Add Contact to continue.

5 If the user is already signed up to Live Messenger, they'll get this prompt when they next log on asking if they want to allow you to see them online and also add you to their contact list. You will see the same window when someone adds you. Once you've been authorised they'll show up on your list.

6 If the user is not registered they will be sent a message informing them of your attempt to add them. They'll appear offline until they register, log in and allow you as a contact.

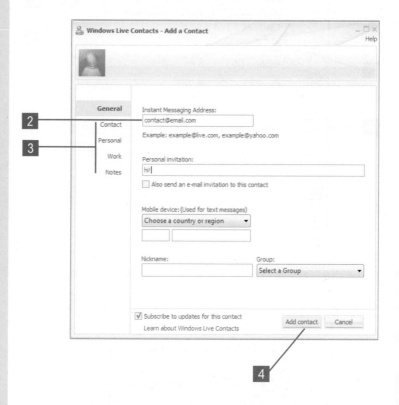

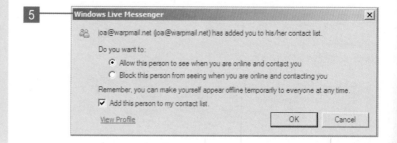

Managing Contacts (cont.)

Delete and block contacts

1 Right-click on a contact, online or off, to see a list of options.

2 Send them an email or message.

3 Messenger includes many extra features such as games, video and voice calling and file sharing that become available when a contact is online.

4 Open the View menu to see a contact card, which many contain more info about the person.

5 Block the contact from seeing you online.

6 Delete a contact to remove them from your contact list – you will no longer be able to message them. When you do this you will be given the option to block them as well.

Chat with Messenger

The main purpose of Live Messenger is, of course, communication. You can open a chat window with any of your online contacts and begin talking to them instantly. You can also send and receive files and play games. Messenger includes a wide range of plugins and extra add-ons you can download to add new animations and features, so you can irritate your friends with smileys and animations or draw silly pictures with the Whiteboard function.

Chat with your contacts

1 Double-click on an online contact to bring up a chat window.

2 Type your messages into the text input box and hit Enter or press Send.

3 The conversation will appear in the main window.

4 Use the icons above the text input to add smileys and other animated icons and emoticons, or change your text font and color.

5 Click the Whiteboard tab to draw pictures. Provided the other person is using a compatible version of Messenger with Whiteboard installed, you can draw and send doodles.

6 Your picture and your contact's picture are shown at the side. Click the lower arrow to change a picture and the side arrow to hide the picture.

7 You can invite other contacts into the chat by clicking Invite then selecting an online contact.

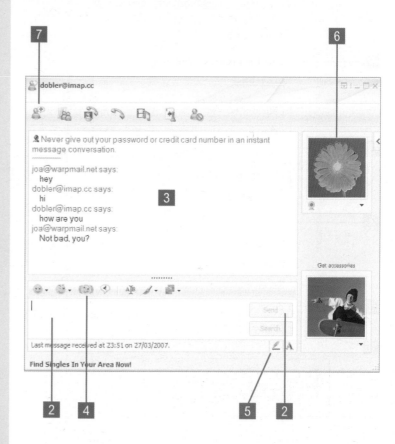

Jargon buster

Emoticons – emotional icons are used in chat to show a particular feeling, like the emotion for happy :) and sad :(. Often referred to as smileys.

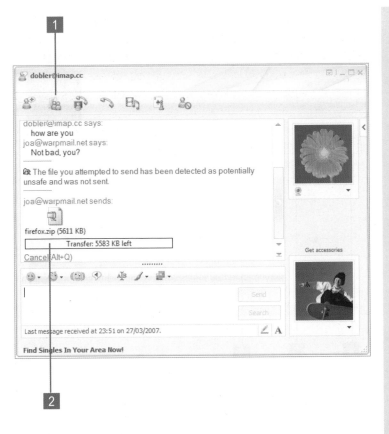

Send files

1 You can send a file by right-clicking in the contact list and going to Send Other then Single File, or click Share Files in an open chat window. Another option is to drag and drop files into the text input area of the chat.

2 If you use the Share Files or Single File option you'll be prompted to locate the file on your computer.

Important !

Be careful about accepting executable files, word documents and other files that could transmit viruses. If the file is coming from someone you don't know and you didn't ask for it, you should check it with your virus scanner. If your virus scanner has an option for watching Instant Messaging enable this as it will help protect against worms that use Instant Messaging to spread.

Sending and receiving files (cont.)

Receive files

1 When receiving a file, you will need to accept it before the transfer will begin.

2 If you click Save As rather than accept, you can save to another location on your hard disk.

3 Click Decline to reject the file.

4 When the file is completed, you can click the link to open it.

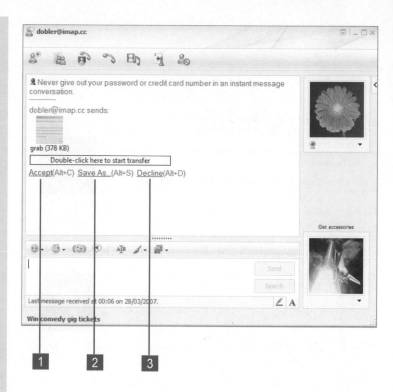

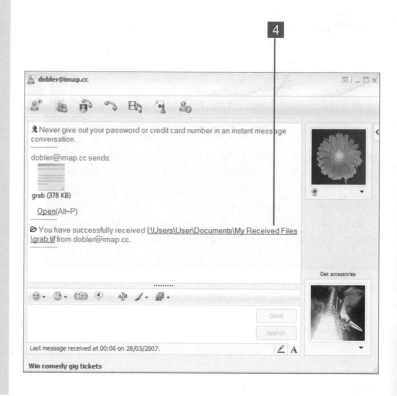

Multimedia

7

Introduction

The main attraction of PCs is their versatility, whether it's browsing the web, working, or playing games. This has really come into play in the last few years as the popularity of digital media has increased rapidly, helped along by the internet, ever-faster broadband connections, digital cameras and DVD video. In this chapter we're going to look at three key areas – images, music and video – and how you can use your PC to view, manage and use your media. Digital cameras are standard issue now. The chances are you've got a rapidly growing collection of images stored on your hard disk, so we'll look at how you view those pictures and also create a slideshow for friends and family (and backing up your precious snaps in the process). Anyone who has shelves bulging with audio CDs should read up on how to digitise albums, allowing you to use them in MP3 players, mobile phones and other devices, as well as creating your own compilations to save wear and tear on the originals. And if you've got a DVD burner and lots of digital videos on your hard disk, the final section of this chapter will tell you about playing video files and DVDs on your computer as well as helping you create your very own DVD disk that can be played back on most standalone players.

What you'll do

View images

Create a DVD slideshow

Listen to music

Listening to streaming Internet radio

Set up Winamp for CD-ripping

Rip audio CDs

Create an audio CD

Play videos and DVDs

Create a DVD

Viewing images

You can view images within Windows without any additional software. Windows Vista now includes Photo Gallery, an image viewer and organisation tool, and that does a perfectly adequate job of browsing your pictures. You can also enable a preview pane for folders so you can see thumbnails of pictures before viewing them in Photo Gallery.

Preview images within folders

1 Locate the folder containing your images, right-click and choose Properties.

2 Click the Customise tab.

3 From the drop-down menu, select Pictures and Videos.

4 You can assign an image to the folder to remind you of its contents, click Choose File to do this.

5 Click Change Icon to select an alternative folder icon.

6 Click Apply.

7 Open the folder.

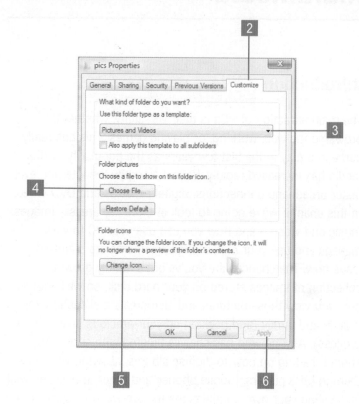

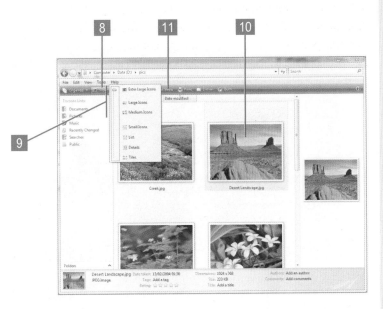

8 In the folder, click the Views menu.

9 If you select medium, large or extra large icons you'll see thumbnails of each picture.

10 Click an image once to display it in the folder, or twice to open it in the associated application.

11 Click the Slideshow button to view a full-screen slideshow of pictures in the current folder.

For your information

Your digital camera images can be transferred to your PC in two ways. First is by using the supplied software and USB cable. Any camera should include even basic applications for transferring, editing and viewing images. Usually some form of simple Photo Editor and a manager/viewer combination that grabs your pictures when you plug in your digicam. The second option is to use a card reader, since the pictures are stored on a removable memory card. Get yourself an inexpensive USB reader (most handle five, six or seven types of memory card) and you can transfer your pics to any system just by dragging and dropping them off the card.

Viewing images (cont.)

View images with Photo Gallery

1 Access Photo Gallery by double-clicking on a picture or, if images are not associated with Photo Gallery, right-clicking and using the Open With menu. You'll also find a shortcut on the Start menu.

2 Use the left and right arrows to move back and forth between the images. You can also use the keyboard cursor keys.

3 Click this button and move the slider to zoom in and out.

4 When you're zoomed in, this button will reset the image to fit the screen.

5 You can rotate images using these buttons but it automatically saves over the original picture. Make sure you've got a backup copy before doing this.

6 This button starts a slideshow.

Timesaver tip

There are specialised applications specifically for viewing images, the most popular of which is ACDSee (www.acdsee.com). Not only does ACDSee offer an easy way to view your images but it also acts as a photo editor and management tool, so you can keep track of all your pictures.

So you've got hundreds of photos taken with a digital camera on your PC. What now? You can print them out, but good quality paper and printer ink is expensive. One of the best ways to show off your holiday snaps is to create a slideshow on CD or DVD that friends and relations can play through their TV or computer. For this, we'll be using CyberLink's PowerProducer, a simple multimedia tool that is often found bundled with digital cameras, printers, PC systems and DVD drives. You can download a trial from www.gocyberlink.com but you may have a full version already.

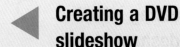

Creating a DVD slideshow

Select a disk type and images

1 From the main menu, choose Produce Movie disk.

2 Now choose a disk type and size. We're going to be creating a DVD and unless you're using a double-layer disk the capacity will be 4.7GB. VCD can be used if you just want to use a CD – most DVD players can also play video CDs – but you're unlikely to need the Blu-Ray or HD-DVD options.

3 For the aspect ratio, select 4:3 if you have a standard television or 16:9 if you're going to play your slideshow on a widescreen display.

4 In the next step click Photos from the Import menu. The interface will change to show the photo slideshow controls.

5 A browse window will open automatically. Locate the folder containing your images and select any you want to include.

6 Click Open and the photos will be added to your slideshow.

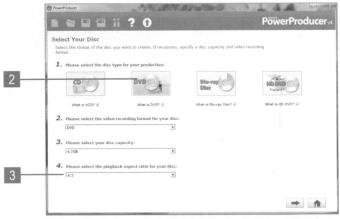

Creating a DVD slideshow (cont.)

Edit your slideshow

1 Your images will now be loaded into the slideshow. You can drag and drop to change their position.

2 Right-click on the album in the filmstrip to view its properties and change its name.

3 Change the display duration of each slide and the entire album. If you leave the album duration blank the slideshow will loop indefinitely.

4 Select a transition effect from the drop-down menu to add a bit of glitz to your slideshow.

5 Check the Back up photos option if you want the original pictures to be saved on the disk as well.

6 Use these playback controls to view a preview of your slideshow.

7 Click to set the currently selected image as the cover image for the album.

8 Watch this meter to ensure that you don't exceed the maximum capacity for your disk.

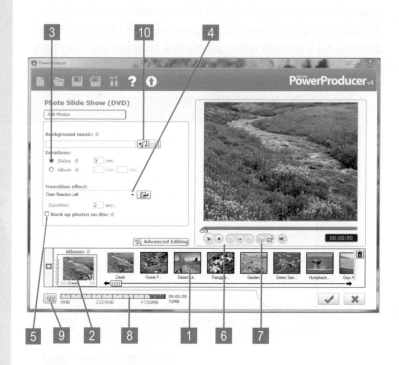

For your information

Windows Vista Home Premium and Ultimate users already have an application for creating slideshows. DVD Maker is now bundled with these versions of Windows Vista and it allows you to burn your photos to a DVD without any additional software. It lacks the extra features of programs such as PowerProducer but is perfectly adequate for basic purposes.

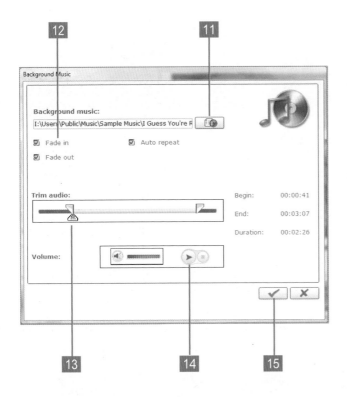

9 View information about the album, such as file size.

10 Click to add background audio to your slideshow.

11 Click Browse and locate the audio track you want to use as background music.

12 Click the boxes to have a fade in, fade out and auto-repeat the track.

13 Use the sliders and drag them up and down to trim the beginning and end of the track.

14 Preview the audio with the playback controls.

15 Click to confirm and save the changes.

16 You'll be taken back to the Slide Show interface. Click the green tick to continue to the next step.

Creating a DVD slideshow (cont.)

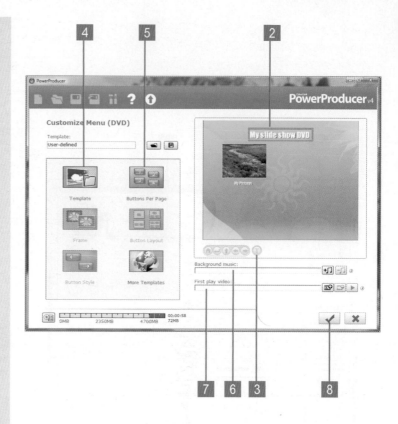

Edit the main menu

1 Back in the menu preview, click the Menu button from the Edit section.

2 Use this screen to customise your main menu. Click the menu text in the preview window and change it to anything you like.

3 Click to select a different font, colour and text size.

4 You can select an alternative Template by clicking this button and selecting one from the gallery.

5 It's also possible to change the button layout. In the trial version the number of changes you can make to the menu and the templates available is limited.

6 Select a background soundtrack to play for the menu.

7 The first-play video will show up before the menu each time the disk is loaded. Using this you can insert your own notices and copyright warnings, serious or otherwise.

8 Save the changes and exit the menu editor.

Important

With options like background music and video it's tempting to add it all to your disk. Don't go overboard though – you'll get fed up of hearing that song loop for the fifth time on a lengthy slideshow. If you're going to put background music on your slideshow go for something subtle and appropriate, and use multiple albums with different audio tracks on each.

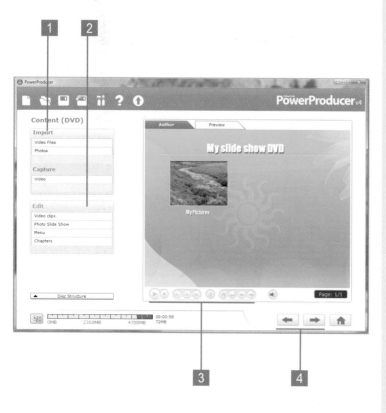

Creating a DVD slideshow (cont.)

Add to the disk

1 To add more albums to your disk, click an option from the Import menu. You can then repeat the album creation process and include multiple chapters.

2 Click an Edit option to edit a particular aspect of your disk.

3 Preview your disk with the playback controls. Click on a chapter then click Play.

4 Click the Next button to finish or back to go back a step.

7

Creating a DVD slideshow (cont.)

Burn the disk

1 Make sure the correct drive is selected. Click Configure to choose an alternative optical drive.

2 If the disk is a re-writable CD or DVD, click the Erase disk content to clear it.

3 Enter a name for your disk. This can be anything up to sixteen characters in length.

4 Check Burn to disk to burn your slideshow straight to a CD or DVD. You can also set how many copies you want to create.

5 If you select the Disk image option, your slideshow will be saved as an image to the hard drive.

6 Create a DVD folder to save your slideshow as raw DVD files. These can then be burnt to disk using any standard disk burning tool, such as Nero Burning ROM or Easy CD.

7 Click the Browse buttons to select a location on your hard disk for the disk image and DVD folder, when applicable.

8 Click to finalise the settings and commit your slideshow to a disk.

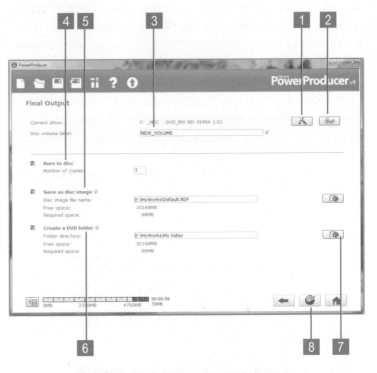

Jargon buster

Disk image – a single file that contains the entire contents of a CD or DVD. You can burn copies safe in the knowledge that each duplicate will be identical.

ID3 tag – part of every MP3 is given over to holding data about the track, like title, artist, year and genre. This is the ID3 tag. It's used by MP3 players, hardware and software, to display information about a file.

Kbps – Kilobits per second, used in reference to audio files to measure the quality of a track. 128kbps is considered CD quality but music fans claim they can hear the difference and prefer songs to be encoded as high as possible. As you increase the kbps the file size also gets larger.

MP3 – MPEG audio layer 3, the most popular digital audio format thanks to its ability to compress audio tracks to a fraction of their size without losing too much of the quality.

Windows Vista comes ready to play back the most common types of audio files. You can use Windows Media Player, but it's a rather bloated and awkward bit of software, so of course we're going to be using an alternative. Winamp is a powerful, feature-packed and slick jukebox that's considered to be the best media player tool for the PC. It can be downloaded for free from www.winamp.com. You can also upgrade to a Pro version which gives you some extra features, most notably the option to convert audio CDs to MP3. Winamp also makes it easy to edit the ID3 tag information of MP3s and organise your music collection with its Media Library.

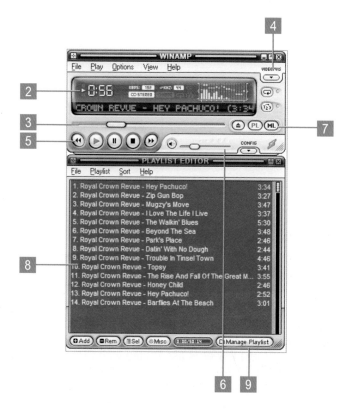

◀ Listening to music

Play music with Winamp

1 Double-click on an MP3 or any other audio file and, assuming it's associated, it will open in Winamp. You can use 'Open With' to open with Winamp otherwise.

2 The top window shows information about the song playing, including information on Kbps and KHz.

3 Drag this slider to change the position of the track.

4 Bring up the visualizer/video window. Visualizer displays an animation that moves in time to your music.

5 Audio playback controls.

6 Change the volume with this slider.

7 Click PL to view and hide the playlist window. ML opens up Media Library, which can be used to catalogue your songs.

Listening to music (cont.)

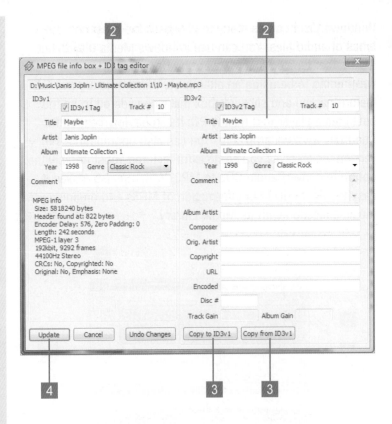

8 This is your playlist. Songs that are currently playing or queued will be listed. You can add songs to the playlist by dragging and dropping from anywhere on your PC. Change their position in the playlist by dragging tracks to where you want them.

9 Click Manage Playlist to Save, Clear or open a new playlist. Change the size of the window by dragging the corner.

Edit track information

1 Right-click on a file in your playlist and choose View File Info.

2 Enter the relevant information into the fields for either ID3v1 or v2. It's best to do both so your songs will display best in devices that support one or the other.

3 Save time by using the Copy to and Copy from buttons to transfer information from one field to another.

4 Click Update to save the information.

For your information

Audio CDs are associated to a program like a normal audio file. When you insert an audio disk Windows will ask whether you want to open it and what program you wish to use. Media Player is associated with CDs by default but Winamp can take over when it's installed.

216

Internet radio has grown to be a huge phenomenon and, in a situation not dissimilar to the infamous pirate radio of the 1980s, has developed from an amateur hobby to full commercial venture. In the early days, stations were operated by individuals using standard PC equipment, broadcasting to a small number of users in a forum or chat room. But as the popularity of streaming audio grew, traditional stations entered the fray, using the web to distribute their shows globally, or specialised companies have sprung up offering home users a hassle-free method of becoming DJs. The most well-known of these is Live365.com, a service that offers an enormous range of stations covering every conceivable taste at a very reasonable price. You can pay for full membership, but the standard free membership lets you listen for nothing, if you don't mind a slightly lower quality and the occasional advert.

Listening to streaming Internet radio

Search Live365

1 Open your web browser and go to www.live365.com.

2 Type the genre of music or type of broadcast you're after into the search field.

3 You can also browse genres by selecting one from the list.

4 Once you've signed up for an account, enter your login details here. You must be a member to listen to stations, but you don't have to join if you're just browsing.

7

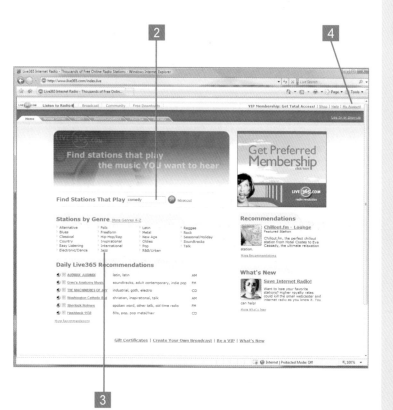

Listening to streaming Internet radio (cont.)

5 When you search you'll see a list of all the stations that match the criteria.

6 Click the speaker icons to open the player window. The gold VIP icons indicate a station that is available to paying members only.

6

For your information

Shoutcast is a technology developed by Nullsoft, the people behind Winamp, that allows anyone to become a DJ. You can use the free software to broadcast from home or listen to thousands of amateur stations worldwide using Winamp. Click over to www.shoutcast.com to find out more.

Use the Live365 Player

1 The track currently playing is highlighted, and the player will also show you the previous track.

2 Click to add the track to your wish list. You can view further information on saved tracks by clicking the wish list button.

3 Rate the track. This helps the station operator know what's popular.

4 Standard Play and Stop buttons for controlling the playback.

5 Control the volume.

6 Add the station to your favourites so you can access it quicker in the future.

For your information

At the time of writing, the Firefox web browser isn't compatible with Live365. However, when the player window opens you'll be asked if you want to open or download a .PLS file. This is a standard playlist file and if you open this in Winamp you can listen to the radio broadcast. This actually works out better, because if you save it to your hard disk you can listen whenever you want without having to go through the website, just by opening the file.

Setting up Winamp for CD-ripping

Set encoder options

1. Open Winamp, go to Options, Preferences and then CD Ripping.

2. Choose an encoder. We're going to use WMA since it's widely supported.

3. Set the Encoder Format to Windows Media Audio 9.2.

4. These options affect the quality of the audio file. The lower the bitrate and sample format, the smaller the file, but the worse it sounds. Unless space is at a premium, we'd recommend using 16-bit stereo 44100Hz sample format and CBR, 320008 bitrate, which will give you larger, but much higher quality, music files.

5. Save your settings.

If you've got a portable audio player or want to listen to your music collection without constantly swapping disks, converting your albums to digital audio files is the only way to go. Using any of the countless CD 'ripping' applications you can extract the audio from a compact disk and convert it to the digital format, which can then be played back on every popular portable audio player or computer system. Once your collection is converted not only is it easy to catalogue and manage your songs, but you save wear and tear on the precious originals stored safely in their jewel cases. We'll be using Winamp to accomplish this. Although you must register the program to create MP3 audio tracks, you can rip to WMA and AAC using the 'Full' free version of Winamp. Although it lacks the advanced options found in a specialised application, Winamp is incredibly easy to use.

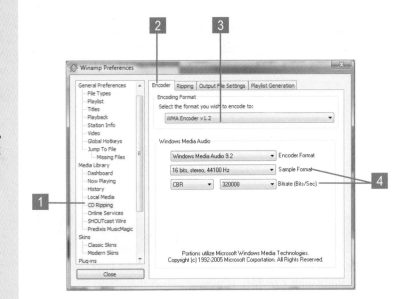

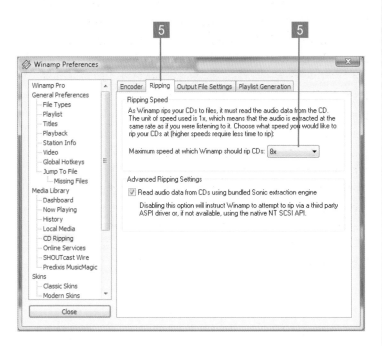

5   **5**

Winamp Preferences

| Winamp Pro | Encoder | Ripping | Output File Settings | Playlist Generation |

Ripping Speed

As Winamp rips your CDs to files, it must read the audio data from the CD. The unit of speed used is 1x, which means that the audio is extracted at the same rate as if you were listening to it. Choose what speed you would like to rip your CDs at (higher speeds require less time to rip):

Maximum speed at which Winamp should rip CDs: 8x

Advanced Ripping Settings

☑ Read audio data from CDs using bundled Sonic extraction engine

Disabling this option will instruct Winamp to attempt to rip via a third party ASPI driver or, if not available, using the native NT SCSI API.

General Preferences
File Types
Playlist
Titles
Playback
Station Info
Video
Global Hotkeys
Jump To File
Missing Files
Media Library
Dashboard
Now Playing
History
Local Media
CD Ripping
Online Services
SHOUTcast Wire
Predixis MusicMagic
Skins
Classic Skins
Modern Skins

Close

Setting up Winamp for CD-ripping (cont.)

5 In the Ripping tab you can set the read speed. This is limited in the free version.

7

Jargon buster

AAC – Advanced Audio Coding, an audio format that is used most notably by Apple for its iPod audio players.

WMA – Windows Media Audio. Competing digital audio format developed by Microsoft. WMA can include DRM so is a popular format for online stores selling music downloads. Most players support WMA (though some can't read its DRM) but one notable exception is Apple's iPod range.

DRM – Digital Rights Management refers to technology used by publishers and copyright owners to control access to and usage of digital material. It can also refer to restrictions associated with a specific instance of a digital work or device.

Setting up Winamp for CD-ripping (cont.)

Select output settings

1 Click Output File Settings.

2 Select a folder for your ripped files by clicking Browse.

3 Specify how you want tracks to be named. Click Format Help to see more information.

4 Select whether ripped files should be added to the Winamp Media Library.

5 This option will add data about the track to the ID3 tag.

6 Type in a comment to be added to the comments field of all your songs.

7 Click Playlist Generation.

8 Choose what playlist files you wish to create for your ripped songs.

9 Choose a name for your playlists in the same way as you did for the tracks themselves.

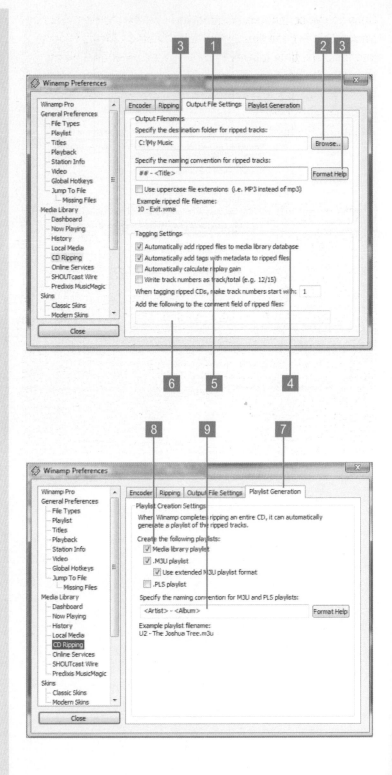

Once you've configured Winamp you can start to rip the audio tracks. This is done simply through Winamp's Media Library interface. The time it takes to rip will vary depending on the speed you've configured through Winamp, the number of tracks you're ripping and the speed of your optical drive. Once it's done, you'll have a complete digital copy of your album waiting on the hard disk.

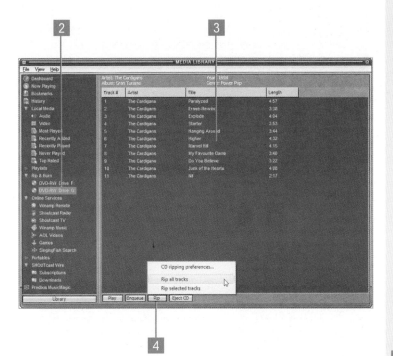

Ripping an audio CD

Rip a CD with Winamp

1. Bring up Media Library by clicking the ML button on Winamp's main interface.

2. In the sidebar, choose the optical drive containing your audio CD from the rip & burn list.

3. If it hasn't already, Winamp will connect to the CDDB and download information about the album.

4. Click the rip button and select Rip selected tracks or Rip all tracks.

Jargon buster

CDDB – Compact Disk Database. Many audio players, such as Winamp, use the online Gracenote CDDB to automatically gather song information. There is also a free competitor, the freedb (www.freedb.org)

Ripping an audio CD (cont.)

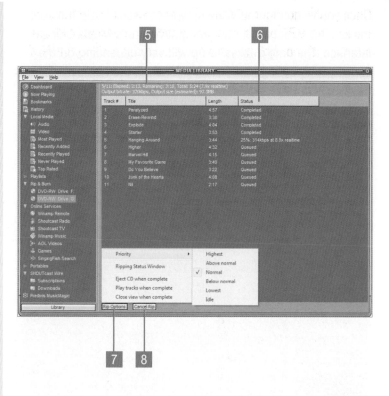

5 Information about the rip is displayed at the top of the screen, including the estimated file size.

6 The Status column shows which tracks are completed, queued or in progress.

7 Click Rip Options to change preferences for the current rip. Setting the priority will tell the system how important it is and therefore how much of its resources it should dedicate to the task.

8 If necessary, you can cancel the rip.

Important

Disk drives can be extremely sensitive to dust and marks on a CD. If your drive has problems reading a track you'll notice popping, hisses and even gaps in the song when it's played back. Make sure the disk is clean before ripping to ensure you get the best quality possible.

Once you've got your albums digitised, you can download them to an MP3 player or listen to them through your PC. In addition, it's possible to create your own audio CDs, which is really useful if you want to make a compilation of favourite tracks or have a backup of an album that you can safely leave in the car. This is incredibly easy to accomplish since every major CD/DVD burning application around now includes the ability to make a CD from digital audio files. We're going to do this using Nero Burning ROM, one of the most popular disk creation tools around.

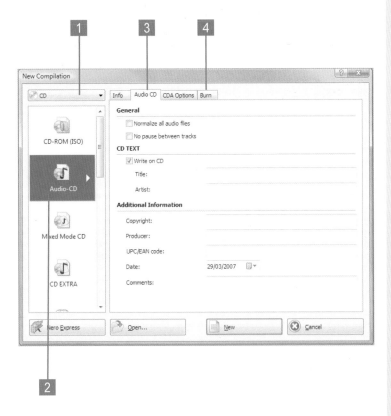

Creating an audio CD

Select disk options

1 Start Nero, and from the New Compilation wizard choose the CD option from the drop-down menu.

2 Select Audio CD.

3 You can enter CD Text information in these fields. This can be read by some CD players.

4 Click the Burn tab.

7

Creating an
audio CD (cont.)

5 Use Simulation to check that the disk will burn correctly.

6 If using Simulation, you can disable Write so that the disk will not be written when the simulation is successful. Otherwise, leave it enabled.

7 Check Finalise if it is not selected.

8 Choose a write speed. If you have problems burning try using a lower setting. Leave the write method on the default selection.

9 Enter the number of copies you wish to make.

10 If Buffer underrun is available and not selected, check this box.

11 When you're finished selecting the options for the disk, click New.

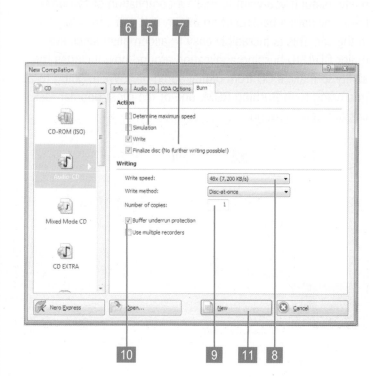

Add your tracks

1 Locate the folder containing your music.

2 Select the songs you want to add to your new CD and drag them into the disk window on the left.

3 Watch the bar at the bottom of the screen. This tells you how much of the disk you've taken up. If it goes yellow, it means you're dangerously close to full capacity and it may not be able to fit everything onto the disk. If it turns red, that means you've gone past maximum capacity.

4 Select songs in the disk window and press Delete to remove them from the compilation. This will not remove them from your hard disk.

5 If you have more than one CD/DVD burner, check that the correct burner is selected.

6 Click to finish and burn the disk. The disk that's created is a standard audio CD and can be used in the majority of CD and DVD players.

Important

If the burn is successful but the disk doesn't work, there can be several reasons. First of all you might be using cheap media. Brand-name blank CDs are of a far higher quality and have better compatibility – poor media is a common cause of burns failing to complete. It could also be the drive, though, as not every CD player can read CD-R disks, so try it in a few other players before binning the disk.

Playing video files

Windows comes equipped with Media Player, so it can handle common video formats out of the box. It's not quite that simple, of course, since there are many different types of video files available and if you download a video file from the Internet there's a good chance it won't work until you install the correct software. You don't have to use Windows Media Player either, there's no shortage of alternate media players that offer all kinds of useful extras. We've used the excellent VLC Media Player, a free open-source application which can be downloaded from www.videolan.org. It looks simple, but has many powerful features, including the ability to play videos without additional software, and even play back files that are damaged or partially downloaded.

1 Double-click on a video file or choose Open With and select the application you wish to use to view the video. For this example, we're using VLC media player.

2 Standard playback controls for play, pause and stop. Click the eject icon to open a file.

3 Use the buttons on the far left and far right of these four to go back and forward in a playlist. The two in the middle control the playback speed.

4 Change the volume.

5 The viewer window, where your video is displayed. Double click this to expand the video to full screen.

6 Jump back and forward in a video using this slider.

Timesaver tip

Find out what codecs a file is using by downloading G-Spot from www.headbands.com/gspot. Don't mind the slightly rude name, G-Spot is a great little tool that examines video files and tells you exactly what codec they're using, so you can check files you've downloaded and then search online for the correct codec if it's needed.

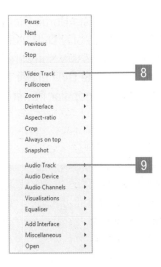

7 Right-click on the viewer window to bring up a list of options.

8 Use video track to switch video streams, when applicable. If the video has subtitles, they will appear as an additional option.

9 The audio track option allows you to select an alternative audio track

Important

Like digital audio files, videos come in many different formats. Although you can play basic WMV and MPG movies through Windows, you'll need to download alternative codecs to play others. Many .AVI video files use the Divx (www.divx.com) or Xvid (www.xvid.org) codecs and while Windows Media Player can open these, they won't be displayed correctly without the software. If you download a video and get sound without a picture or vice versa, it's probably because you have a missing codec. The best option is a codec pack, which bundles common codecs and utilities into one package. For playing videos, we'd recommend the Combined Community Codec Pack (CCCP) which can be downloaded from www.cccp-project.net.

Jargon buster

Codec – COmpressor DECompressor. A codec, such as MP3 or Divx, not only provides the capability to decompress (or decode) files for viewing, but also compress (encode) for creating audio and video.

Divx – popular codec that compresses video without losing too much quality. Gained some notoriety after it was widely used to distribute movies over the Internet.

WMV – Windows Media Video. Digital video format developed by Microsoft.

Xvid – an open-source video codec, has overtaken Divx recently as the format of choice for sending video over the Internet.

Playing DVD movies

If you've got Windows Vista Home Premium or Ultimate you already have the ability to play DVD videos with Windows Media Player as the necessary software is included. Everyone else will require a separate DVD player application. For this example we've used the popular PowerDVD.

1 PowerDVD, or your assigned DVD player, will open when you insert a DVD movie disk.

2 In the playback controls, the first two sets of arrow icons move you forward and back through the chapters, the second set allow you to go back and forward one frame at a time.

3 This button opens the menu options.

4 This button allows you to switch off or swap between subtitles.

5 To swap between audio streams, when available, click this button.

6 Take a screen grab. The captured file is copied to the clipboard and can be pasted into an image editor.

7 You can speed up or slow down the video with this button. You can also do this with your mouse wheel.

8 Use this button to adjust the volume.

9 Open PowerDVD configuration.

Important

If you want to play DVDs from a different region, you'll either need to set the region manually or use a software application to disable it. You can find out how to set the DVD region in Chapter 5, but if you regularly play foreign disks it's far easier to use a program like DVD Region Free (www.dvdidle.com) which disables the region and saves you having to set a region on your drive permanently.

We've shown you how to make a slideshow and your own audio disks, so how about your very own DVD? To do this, we'll again be using PowerProducer, the same application used to build a photo slideshow. We selected photos before, so this time we use the Import Video option. Easy! PowerProducer includes some basic options for editing the videos, so you can cut sections, merge clips into one or split them into multiple parts. And of course you can customise your DVD interface as well, making a fully-functional DVD menu that'll work in any player.

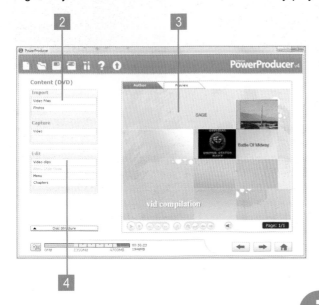

Creating a DVD

Select your disk content

1 Following the same steps as we used in the photo slideshow tutorial, open PowerProducer, select Produce Movie Disk from the menu, then choose DVD and set the size of your disk (4.7 GB in most cases).

2 In the Content menu, choose Import Video. Then select the video files you wish to add to your disk.

3 The selected files will be imported and placed in the menu.

4 From the Edit menu, click Video Clips.

For your information

There are two sizes of DVD disks available – 4.7 GB single-layer and 8 GB dual-layer. Newer DVD burners can handle the dual-layer format and allow you to burn almost double the amount of data. To do this you must have a compatible 8 GB blank disk. To make matters even more confusing, you must also contend with + and – DVD formats. The two types are competing formats from companies that couldn't agree on a single standard back when DVDs were first released. Initially, drives could only handle one or the other, which led to much anger from customers as they bought media for one that didn't work on their single-format drive. All new drives now handle both formats, so as long as you've got a relatively new DVD burner, you don't need to worry about which type you buy.

Creating a DVD (cont.)

Cut your video clips

1 Select a clip from the filmstrip.

2 Move the sliders on the preview so that they're between the content you want to remove.

3 Click Delete selected.

4 Press Cut to delete.

5 Click to set the current frame as the thumbnail.

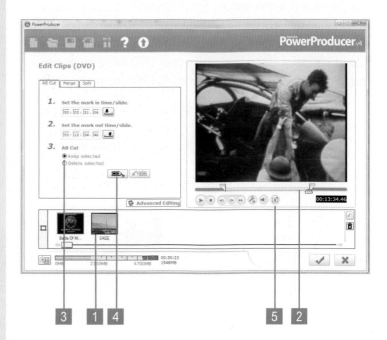

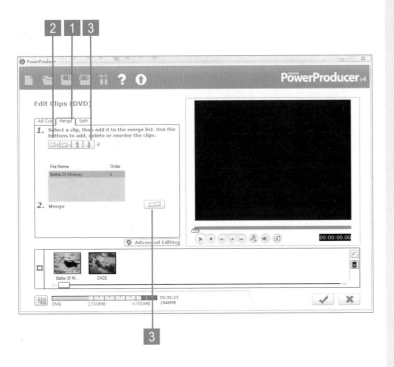

Merge video clips

1 Click the Merge tab.

2 Use the plus icon to add the selected video clip to the merge queue.

3 Use the arrow buttons to change the order of selected clips.

4 Click the Merge button to join the two clips into one.

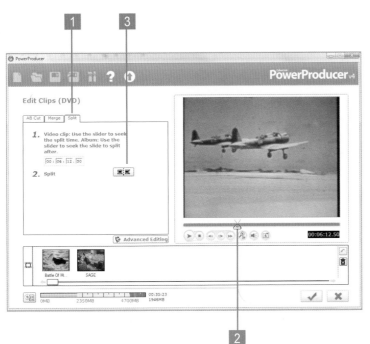

Split video files

1 Click the Split tab.

2 Move the slider on the preview to the point where you wish to split the video.

3 Click the Split button and one video will become two.

7

Finalising and burning your DVD

Once you've finished adding and editing your video files it's time to customise the interface and commit the contents to a disk. Use the templates to choose a look for your menu and also select a button layout. When that's done, you can create the final product. While usually you'll want to burn to disk straight away, we're going to use the 'DVD Folder' option. This places the files that make up a DVD onto your hard disk, where they can then be burnt to a disk as many times as you like using PowerProducer or any disk-burning application, such as Nero. This is useful to know for the future, in case you ever extract the contents of a DVD to your hard disk or download a DVD.

Edit and test the menu

1. If you wish to change the template or button styles, click Menu from the Edit section.

2. To add more video, or even include a photo slideshow, click an option from the Import menu.

3. Click the Preview tab to view your disk as it will appear in DVD players.

4. Ensure that you do not go over the maximum file size for your disk type.

5. Click the Next arrow to go to the final step.

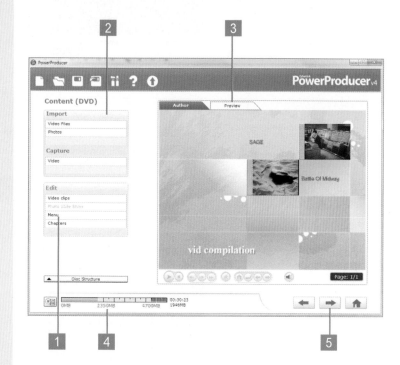

Finalising and burning your DVD (cont.)

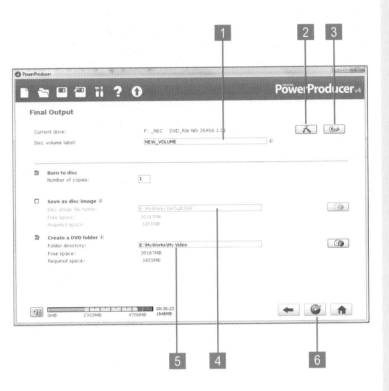

Finish your DVD

1 If you're burning straight to disk, ensure that you have a blank disk and that the correct drive is selected.

2 Click the Configure button to choose another optical drive and change the burn speed.

3 If the disk is a re-writable, click here to erase it. Note that a number of drives and players have problems with re-writable media, so it's preferable not to use this for video compilations.

4 You can save the DVD to your hard disk as an image.

5 For the purposes of this tutorial, we're going to use the Create a DVD folder option. If you just want to commit straight to disk, select Burn to disk.

6 Click Burn to begin creating your DVD.

Finalising and burning your DVD (cont.)

Burn the DVD files

1 Go back to PowerProducer's main menu and select Disk Utilities.

2 If you have saved a DVD as image, you can use the Burn From Image to create a disk.

3 This menu also includes the option for copying a DVD.

4 Click Burn Disk from DVD Folder.

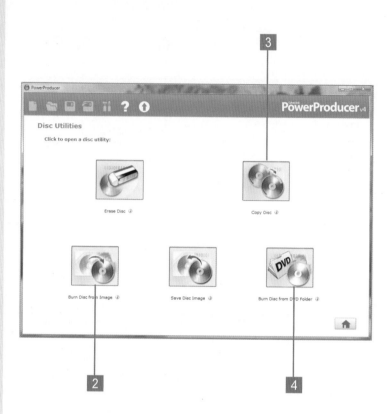

For your information

The Copy Disk option will allow you to copy a DVD, but it will not work for the majority of commercial disks. Duplicating a commercial disk is a copyright violation and the DVD copying tool will not allow you to bypass the protection that's in place on most disks. There are applications, such as DVD Region Free, that include settings for stripping copy protection from a disk when it's inserted into the drive, but copyright owners have begun to crack down on the companies selling them.

Finalising and burning your DVD (cont.)

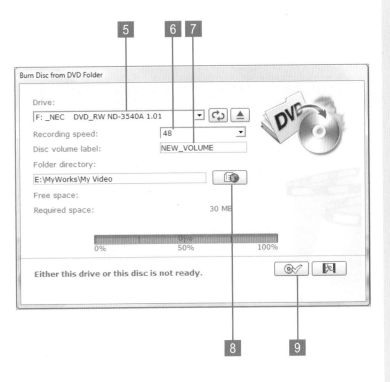

5 Check that you have the correct optical drive selected.

6 Set the recording speed.

7 You can edit the name of the disk.

8 Click Browse and select the folder where your DVD files are located.

9 Click the Burn button to create your DVD from the files.

For your information

Another extra feature for Windows Vista Home Premium and Ultimate owners is Windows DVD Maker, a new application which lets you create DVDs with menus just like PowerProducer. It's not quite as powerful but has the advantage of being totally free and unrestricted, whereas the trial version of PowerProducer has a 30-minute limit on videos.

Maintenance

Introduction

As with any machine, your computer requires regular care and attention to keep it in working order. Unlike a car you don't need to worry about MOTs and road tax but you could have huge amounts of valuable data stored on your hard drive, so taking good care of your system will ensure that data remains safe. As well as basic system housekeeping like regularly emptying the Recycle Bin, deleting unused programs and ensuring you have sufficient security, you should use the built-in disk maintenance tools to defragment and fix your drives. There is little you can do about catastrophic hard disk failure as it can occur without warning due to mechanical failure, but you can use these tools to minimise the danger of your files becoming corrupted. It's also vital that you insure yourself against disaster, so we're going to look at the WinZip file compression utility and Windows own backup features. WinZip allows you to create and view compressed archives, which are often used for distributing files on the Internet, so it helps to know how to use it even if you never make the zip files yourself.

What you'll do

Back up your files and folders

Back up your computer

Restore your files

Adjust back up settings

Create compressed archives

Use System Restore

Defragment your hard drive

Clean up and check your hard disk

Maintain your hardware

Safeguarding your files with Windows Backup

Back up, back up, back up. This is one of the basic rules of computing. Hard disks can and probably will fail at some point and you will lose your data. If there are no backups you've got nobody to blame but yourself. There's no excuse either since Windows Vista includes its own backup feature. There is no shortage of free and commercial software that does the same thing of course, but since you already have Vista's and it will fulfil most users needs it's worth learning how to use it before you consider buying a new package. You can use it to save individual files and folders or perform a complete disk backup for quick and easy restoration.

Using the Backup and Restore Centre

1. To access the Windows backup features, open the Control Panel. If you're using the Classic View, double-click Backup and Restore Centre, or in the Control Panel Home view click Back up your computer. The Backup Centre is a central point for all backup and restore options, including file and hard disk backup and the System Restore feature.

2. In Windows XP the System Restore feature was accessed via Windows Help, but it's now situated here. Use the options in the task menu to create a new restore point or recover from a previous saved state.

3. These two options allow you to make backups of individual files or a complete hard disk.

4. After you've created a new backup use the restore functions to recover your files or hard drives.

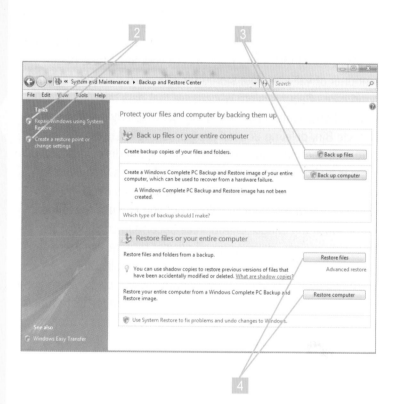

Jargon buster

Wizard – a simplified program interface that makes it easier for beginners to use the application. Although wizard modes often have fewer features available they're much quicker if you just want to run a basic task.

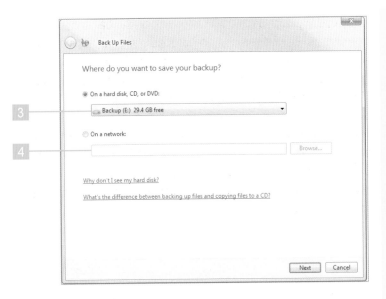

Safeguarding your files with Windows Backup (cont.)

Back up files

1. Click the Back Up Files button.

2. There will be a pause while Windows searches for suitable locations to store your backup. This will include hard drives (internal and external), DVD and CD writers and removable memory devices. Windows Vista Home Premium and Ultimate users also have the option of saving to other systems on the same network.

3. If you want to save to a hard disk or optical drive check this option and choose the target drive from the drop-down menu. Make sure you have enough free memory on whatever drive you select.

4. It's also possible to save to a network location with some versions of Windows Vista. When you select this option you'll have to browse your network and choose a suitable location on an accessible system.

5. Click Next to continue.

8

Safeguarding your files with Windows Backup (cont.)

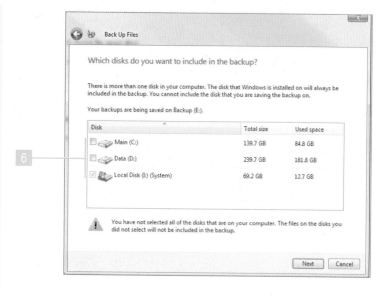

6 In this step you need to select which hard disks are going to be included in the backup. Take note of the used space on each drive, if you're backing up a large amount of data you should ensure the destination drive has enough free space.

7 Choose what types of files you want to back up by selecting from these options. Unfortunately you cannot choose specific files or folders, but any files that aren't included in the other categories will be saved by choosing the Documents, Compressed Files and Additional Files options. You can see more information about the categories by holding the mouse over each.

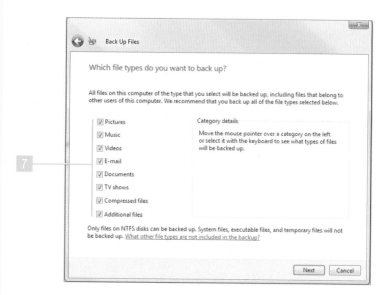

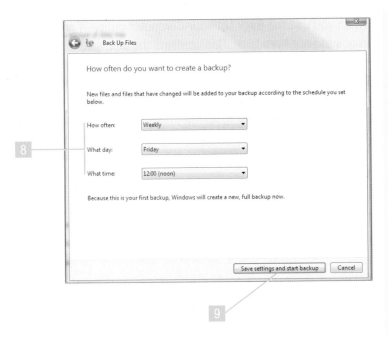

How often do you want to create a backup?

New files and files that have changed will be added to your backup according to the schedule you set below.

How often: Weekly ▼

What day: Friday ▼

What time: 12:00 (noon) ▼

Because this is your first backup, Windows will create a new, full backup now.

Save settings and start backup   Cancel

8

9

8 Finally, you need to set a schedule for the backup. It will then be repeated every week to ensure you've always got up-to-date backups.

9 Click the Save settings button and the initial backup will begin.

8

Back up your computer

▶

When you use the Back Up Your Computer option it creates an image of your hard disk. This contains the entire contents of the drive, including Windows and all necessary system files, so that if you ever need to recover your system you can do it very quickly and easily without having to reinstall your software. The only problem is that the resulting image file can take a huge amount of space so you'll either need to span it across several blank DVDs or make sure you've got plenty of free storage on another hard drive.

1 Select Back Up Computer in the Backup and Restore Centre.

2 Choose whether you'd like to save the image to a hard disk or CD/DVD drive. With the latter it will be necessary to use many blank disks to store the backup file.

3 Now choose which drives are to be backed up. The backup tool will automatically include the drive containing Windows, in this example we actually have two operating systems installed – Windows Vista and an older version of Windows – so the backup has selected these already. Check the boxes to add other drives to the backup.

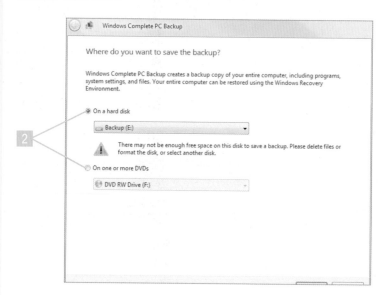

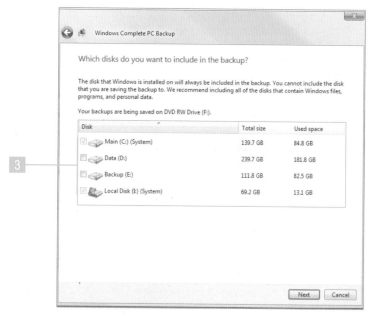

Important

When backing up your files it's vital to think about the media onto which you save them. Using an internal hard disk is very convenient as they offer a great deal of space for very little money, but if you're using the drive on a day-to-day basis it increases the chance of losing all the data if your computer is damaged or lost. To be safe you should use some form of external storage medium. External hard disks are relatively inexpensive and easy to keep hidden out of sight, and when used sparingly and stored safely they usually have a long life. Another popular option is blank CDs and DVDs. These are very cheap but there have been some concerns about the shelf life of optical media and they offer far less space than a hard disk, meaning drive backups must be spanned across multiple disks, increasing the likelihood that the backup will become damaged. They're great for individual files, though, but you should always buy good quality, brand-name disks and keep them out of direct sunlight.

4 You'll be given a summary of the backup before continuing. We chose to backup to a DVD drive, but as you can see this does take a very large number of disks. In most situations it's best to save files to a hard disk with lots of free space, as it's much easier than having to swap and label a pile of DVDs.

5 Click Start backup to begin. The time it takes will vary greatly depending on the transfer and write speed of the device you're saving to and the size of the backup.

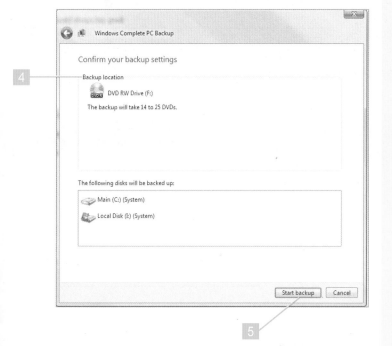

Restoring your files

Restoration of your backup files has been made very simple in Windows Vista. Not only does it store the details of older backups but when you come to restore you can choose exactly which files you want restored, it doesn't just overwrite everything that was backed up previously. Once again this is all accomplished via the Backup and Restore Centre.

1. Open the Backup and Restore Centre.

2. Click the Restore Files button.

3. Windows keeps a record of previous backups as well as the latest, so you can recover from an older file set if necessary. Choose either to use the latest backup or select an older file.

4. If you chose to restore an older backup rather than the very latest, you'll be given a list showing previous backup states. Select one and click Next.

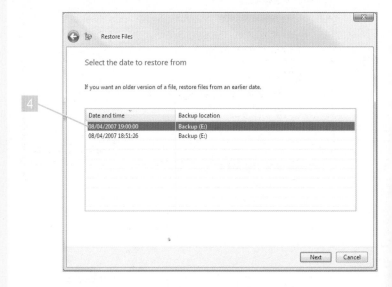

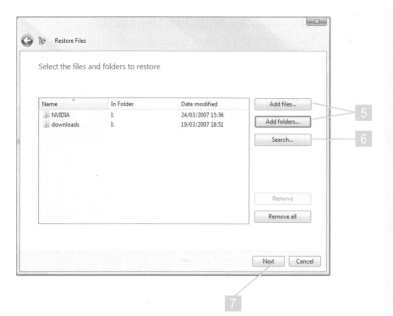

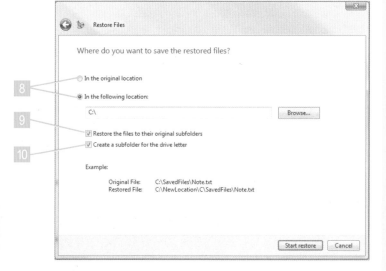

5 Click Add files or Add folders to select files and folders from your backup. When you do this a browser window will appear, showing you the contents of the backup file as though it were a drive on your system.

6 Use the Search option to find a specific file or folder within the backup.

7 Once you've added all the files and folders you want to restore click Next.

8 Now choose whether to restore the files to their original location, which will overwrite the current files, or to a new folder.

9 If you place them in a new location you can retain the original folder names by checking this option.

10 This option organises the backups into folders named after the drive letter of their original location. This is recommended when you're dealing with large numbers of files.

Adjusting backup settings

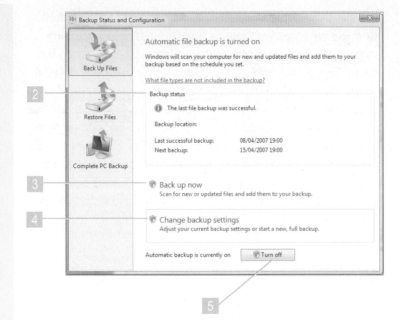

1. When you create a backup schedule you'll notice it will be listed in the Backup and Restore Centre along with a new Change Settings option. Click this to configure the backup.

2. Check when the last backup occurred by reading the backup status.

3. You don't need to wait for the automatic backup – click Back up now to run it straight away.

4. Click Change backup settings to reconfigure your backup.

5. Disable/enable automatic backup.

In order to free up some space on your hard disk without deleting stuff you can make your files take up less space by squashing multiple files into archives. We do this using a compression tool, the most popular of which is WinZip (www.winzip.com). WinZip allows you to make a 'zip' archive, applying varying levels of compression and other options, into which you can drop any type of file. Compression is particularly useful when backing up since you can save space on the backup media. WinZip is one of those essential applications since zip files are used extensively on the Internet for packaging downloads. Windows XP does include the capability to handle them without WinZip, but you'll miss out on lots of useful features.

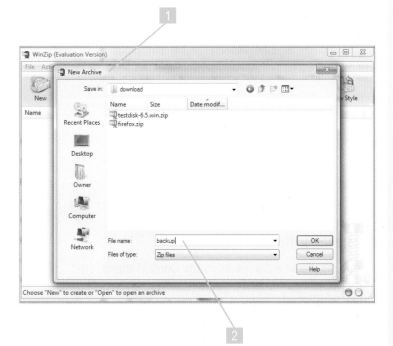

Compressing and archiving your files

Create a new compressed archive

1 Load WinZip and click New.

2 Navigate to the folder in which you want to save the new archive and then enter a filename.

8

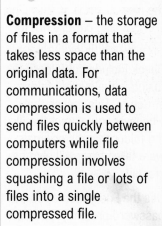

Jargon buster

Compression – the storage of files in a format that takes less space than the original data. For communications, data compression is used to send files quickly between computers while file compression involves squashing a file or lots of files into a single compressed file.

Zip – the most popular data compression format. It was invented by programmer Phil Katz in the '80s for his company PKWARE. He also made the first zip file utility, PKZIP.

For your information

If you download a program from the Internet it will often be compressed into a zip file. Sometimes you can run the set-up directly from the zip without extracting all the files, the set-up routine will do that for you, and in some cases you'll need to extract the files to a folder, run the set-up and then delete the extracted installation files.

Compressing and archiving your files (cont.)

3   Now browse to the folder containing the files you want to archive and select them.

4   Use the action menu to select how you want the program to deal with the files. The default Add (and replace) will overwrite files with the same name.

5   Select the level of compression. Normal is the default, Maximum squashes the files as small as they'll go. You can also choose not to have any compression.

6   Check Include subfolders to maintain the current folder structure. This means that whenever you extract the files the folder that the originals were taken from will also be created.

7   Use the Encryption option to password protect your files. You'll be prompted for a password when you click Add.

8   Check Save path info to retain folder information. When the files are extracted they will then use the original folder names.

9   Add the files to your archive.

Timesaver tip

You can create a zip file from the Context menu. Just right-click in a folder or on the desktop, choose New, then WinZip File. Enter a name for the archive and then open it and add files or simply drag and drop them onto the icon.

For your information

If you select the Maximum (Enhanced Deflate) compression option, you may not be able to open the archive with some older versions of WinZip.

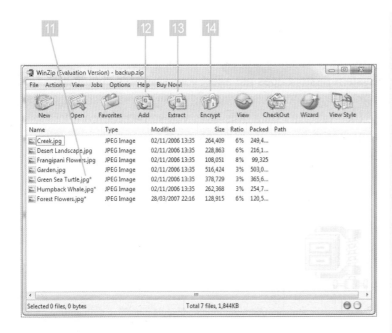

Compressing and archiving your files (cont.)

10 Once your files have been compressed, you'll be taken to the archive.

11 Files with a wildcard (*) are password protected. When you try to open or extract these you'll have to enter the correct password.

12 Add more files to the archive.

13 Click to extract the selected files. You'll be prompted to choose a location for the files. You can also drag and drop files from an archive into a folder but this will remove any folder structure.

14 If you use the Encrypt option here it will protect the whole archive – you cannot select individual files.

8

Important

Don't rely on WinZip for the long-term backup of important files. If a zip archive becomes corrupted you'll lose any data inside them. If you need to back up vital data, consider using a second hard disk, external hard drive or even a RAID 1 (see Jargon buster section) set-up, which will ensure that your system is protected against everything but theft or the complete destruction of your PC. Always keep multiple copies of anything you can't afford to lose.

For your information

Although zip files are the most common type of compressed archive, there are many variations. WinZip can open most of these, but it can't handle RAR files. If you need to open and extract an RAR archive you will need to download WinRAR from www.rarlabs.com.

Use System Restore

Windows includes a System Restore function for recovering a previous configuration in case you make a mistake or a program goes crazy and starts messing with your settings. System Restore does not affect your saved files but it will remove installed applications and change system settings back to their previous state. This gives you some headroom for experimenting with applications, since you can always jump back a step if it all goes wrong. Helpfully, you can also undo the last restore to set the configuration back the way it was.

Set a system restore point

1. Go to the Control Panel and open the Backup and Restore Centre.

2. Click create a restore point in the tasks list.

3. Select the hard disk on which you want to make a restore point.

4. Click Create to start the process.

5. Enter a memorable name for the restore point and click Create to finish.

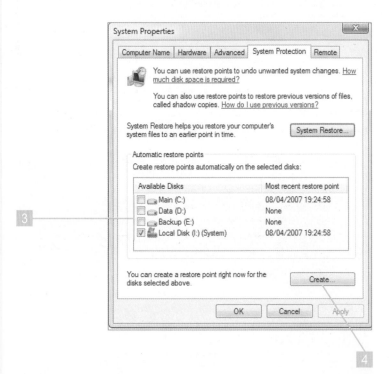

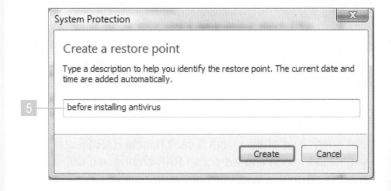

Important

Before installing any application which could potentially affect the system, such as disk and file management programs or tweaking tools, use System Restore and create a backup point. You'll sometimes find that the programs you install have also done this automatically.

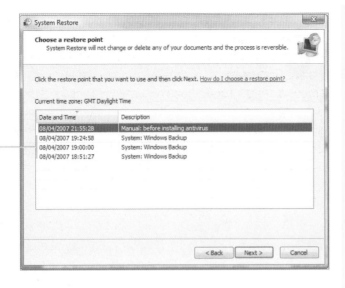

Recover to a previous restore point

1. Click repair windows in the Backup and Restore Centre task list.

2. Select a restore point from the list and click Next.

3. Select the drives you want to restore. The disk containing Windows will be automatically selected.

4. Review the information and check that it's correct, then click Next to finish. Your system will now be rebooted and restored during start-up.

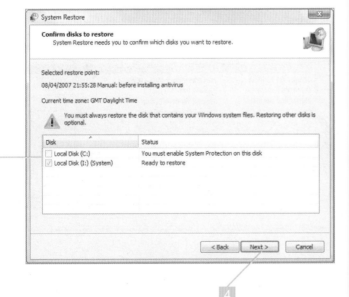

Use System Restore (cont.)

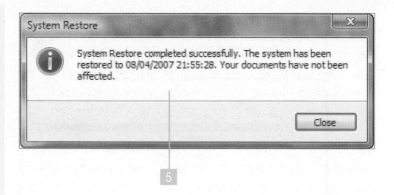

5

5 A notice will be displayed when you reboot, confirming a successful restore procedure.

Undo a restoration

6 If you want to undo the restore process go back to the Repair System option in the Backup and Restore Centre. You'll see a new restore point to undo the changes.

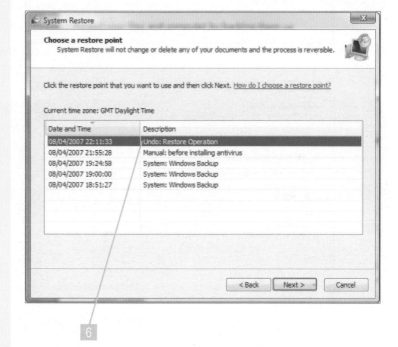

6

Over time the files on your hard disk will become fragmented, causing the drive to work harder to locate data. Fragmentation occurs when a drive splits files into multiple pieces then uses the file system to track the location of the parts on the disk. When asked to access that file it will need to spend time looking for and gathering the scattered data, therefore it's obviously beneficial to ensure that fragmentation is kept to a minimum so your hard disk will work faster. You should run defrag on a regular basis, about once or twice a month. If it's been a while since you defragged you may also need to run it more than once at a time – use the analyse tool to check whether that's necessary.

Defragging a hard disk

Use Defrag to tidy your hard drive

1 Open Disk Defragmenter from the System Tools category in Accessories

2 Click Defragment now to begin the defrag process immediately. It will automatically defrag all your drives.

3 Use this option to enable an automatic defrag, so you don't have to remember to run it yourself.

4 Click Modify schedule to adjust the time and day of the automatic defrag.

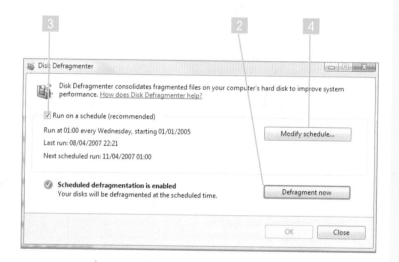

Jargon buster

Defrag – fragmentation is where files are split into multiple parts on a hard disk. When you defrag, the file system joins these parts back together, or at least moves them closer to each other, so that the hard disk has less work to so when searching.

Cleaning up your hard disk

After a while you'll have accumulated quite a large number of junk files on your hard disk. As well as going round manually clearing up the trash, Windows has a small utility that can scan your drive and pinpoint rubbish. It's useful to run this occasionally as it delves into the depths of system folders and may well find a cache of trash that you would have otherwise missed.

Search your hard disk for useless files

1. Open Disk Cleanup from the System Tools menu in Accessories.

2. Select the drive you want to clean and click OK.

3. Disk Cleanup will search the drive looking for files that can be deleted.

4. Check the box next to each type of file you want to clear.

5. Select a file category and check the description that appears to ensure you do not need the files.

6. Click View Files to open the folder containing the selected files.

7. Press OK to delete the checked file types.

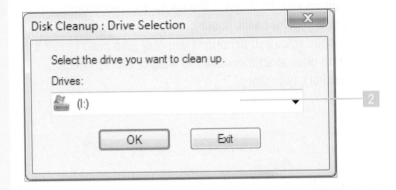

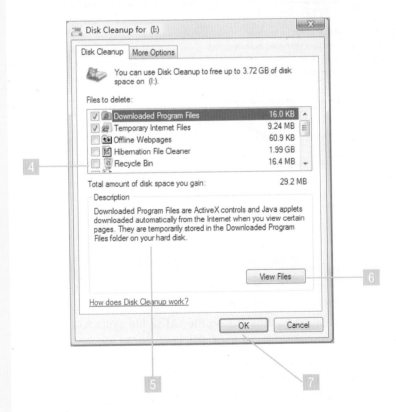

Cleaning up your hard disk (cont.)

8　Click the More Options tab.

9　Click Clean up under Programs and Features to uninstall applications.

10　Use the Restore options Clean up to remove old system restoration points. Make sure you do not need them as there is no way to recover these after they're deleted.

8

Checking your hard disk with CHKDSK

Older versions of Windows and DOS included the Scandisk utility that checked your hard drive for corrupted files and directories. This has now been replaced with CHKDSK. Run from the command prompt, CHKDSK will search for and fix file system inconsistencies which could potentially grow into big problems later on. As with defrag, you should use CHKDSK regularly to keep your hard drive healthy.

1 Click Start, and then Run.

2 Type CHKDSK C: /f /r. This command will check and fix errors on the C drive. If you want to check another drive, replace the C with the letter of a different disk. Be aware that this process can take several hours, depending on the size of your hard disk.

3 CHKDSK will ask you if you want to schedule the operation for a reboot, as it's unable to fix drive errors while the disk is in use. Type Y to agree, N to cancel. If you select yes, the utility will run before Windows starts the next time you switch on your PC.

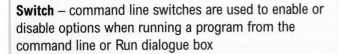

```
I:\Windows\system32\chkdsk.exe
The type of the file system is NTFS.

WARNING!  F parameter not specified.
Running CHKDSK in read-only mode.

CHKDSK is verifying files (stage 1 of 3)...
  51904 file records processed.
File verification completed.
  47 large file records processed.
  0 bad file records processed.
  2 EA records processed.
  60 reparse records processed.
CHKDSK is verifying indexes (stage 2 of 3)...
14 percent complete. (10307 of 201821 index entries processed)
```

4 You can run CHKDSK in read only mode by just running CHKDSK C:

Note that it will not fix errors without using the /F switch.

8

Maintaining your hardware

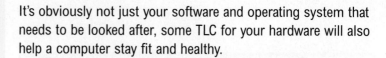

It's obviously not just your software and operating system that needs to be looked after, some TLC for your hardware will also help a computer stay fit and healthy.

■ Case fans, CPU coolers and other internal parts will quickly become clogged with dust. If your case has removable filters you can replace or clean them, otherwise use a can of compressed air and blow the dirt out. Always blow it out of your case, never in and do not use the air directly on the fans as you can damage them.

■ Make sure that all cables inside your PC are tucked out the way. This will help to keep your system cool by improving airflow.

■ Proper cooling is incredibly important as modern components get very hot. If you have a fan hole in your case with no fan fitted, it's a good idea to buy one. Also consider the placement of hardware. For example, hard disks should be as far apart from each other as possible and the same goes for expansion cards. This is especially important when you've got a new graphics card as some of these can get extremely hot, you don't want another card right next to it having all the hot air blown on it.

■ Ensure that all your expansion cards are seated correctly in their slots and that every component and cable is securely screwed down. The last thing you want is for a component to fall out while your PC is being moved or, even worse, in use. Loose expansion cards and cables are a surprisingly frequent culprit of system errors.

Jargon buster

AAC – Advanced Audio Coding, an audio format that is used most notably by Apple for its iPod audio players.

Adware – installed along with other applications and delivers adverts, sometimes through the application window and sometimes through pop-up windows. Often Adware is more of an annoyance than a genuine threat, as many free programs use it to bring in money.

AGP – Accelerated Graphics Port, based on the PCI interface, AGP was developed exclusively for graphics cards, replacing the general-use PCI slot. It's now being phased out in favour of PCI-express, but AGP cards are still being manufactured because of the abundance of AGP systems.

AMD – Advanced Micro Devices, Intel's only real competitor in the CPU market is AMD, who make the extremely popular Athlon and Athlon 64 series of processors.

Anti-static bag – components are usually shipped in grey plastic bags that have been treated to protect against static damage. It's a good idea to hold on to these as they may come in useful when upgrading.

Associations – files are associated with applications so that they will open in that particular program when run. This saves you from manually opening a program each time.

Auto-update – software that auto-updates will download and install the latest version of itself, often without user-intervention. Sometimes called a live update.

AVI – Audio Video Interleave, a Windows video format, used by many different codecs such as Divx.

Bandwidth – the amount of data that can be transmitted within a certain amount of time. For internet connections, this is bps, bytes per second.

BIOS – Basic Input Output System, the software that enables basic functionality of hardware on all systems, whether they have an operating system or not, and allows you to configure hardware settings. The BIOS is stored on a Read-Only Memory (ROM) chip on the motherboard, so will always be available even if the hard disk crashes. You can access your BIOS by hitting the assigned key when your system starts, which is usually Delete.

Bit rate – speed at which data transfers in a certain amount of time. With audio and video files, a higher bit rate means better quality.

Broadband – traditionally the name given to a service which uses a single wire to carry many signals, for example cable telephone services that also provide television. Recently it has been applied to fast internet connections though ISPs will call anything from 256k upwards broadband when many don't believe that is true broadband as it's not fast enough. Most broadband connections now are at least 512k.

CBR – Constant Bit Rate. If an audio file is encoded with CBR, it means the bit rate, and therefore sound quality, is uniform through the entire length of the file. See also: VBR.

CDDB – Compact Disk Database. Many audio players, such as Winamp, use the online Gracenote CDDB to automatically gather song information. There is also a free competitor, the freedb (www.freedb.org)

Codec – COmpressor DECompressor. A codec, such as MP3 or Divx, not only provides the capability to decompress (or decode) files for viewing, but also compress (encode) for creating audio and video.

Compression – the storage of files in a format that takes less space than the original data. For communications, data compression is used to send files quickly between computers while file compression involves squashing a file or lots of files into a single compressed file.

Computer administrator – when applied to user accounts, the administrator account means that person has full access to the entire system, including the ability to install and remove software and other tasks affecting the administration of the system. When we're talking about networks and corporate computer systems, the administrator is the person in charge of maintaining the systems.

Context menu – the term given to the menu that appears when you right-click, so called because its functions change depending on the program or area of the operating system in which you currently reside.

Control Panel – an important area of Windows that contains links to settings and controls for hardware, software and peripherals.

CPU – Central Processing Unit, often called the processor or chip. It's the brain of any system, handling the majority of the calculations.

DDR-RAM – Double Data Rate RAM, the follow-up to SDRAM, this type of memory is currently used in AMD systems.

DDR-2 – the successor to DDR-RAM. Supposedly faster though there's actually little difference between the two types of memory. DDR-2 is currently used only in Intel systems.

Defrag – (defragment) Fragmentation is where files are split into multiple parts around a hard disk. When you defrag, the file system joins these fragmented parts back together, or at least moves them closer to each other, so that the hard disk has less work to do when searching.

Disk image – a single file that contains the entire contents of a disk, be it a CD or DVD. You can then burn copies safe in the knowledge that each duplicate will be identical.

Divx – popular codec that compresses video without losing too much quality. Gained some notoriety after it was widely used to distribute movies over the Internet.

DRM – Digital Rights Management refers to technology used by publishers and copyright owners to control access to and or usage of digital material. It can also refer to restrictions associated with a specific instance of a digital work or device.

Email – electronic mail, messages sent over an electronic network, stored in a server until the recipient reads them.

Emoticons – emotional icons are used in chat rooms to show a particular feeling, like the emoticon for happy :) and sad :(. Often referred to as smileys.

Enclosure – also called a case or chassis, it's the metal frame that holds all your PC components together. Cases come in many sizes for different purposes, though the most common is a midi-desktop tower.

Encryption – the conversion of data into a scrambled code, so that it cannot be read by normal means. Encrypted data must be unscrambled before it can be accessed. Most encryption is not completely foolproof but modern encryption techniques take a large amount of skill and computing power to crack.

EXE – a file with the .EXE extension means that it is an executable program file, a self-contained program that will run on its own. This can be a software installation package or application.

Extension – the letters after a filename that tell you what kind of data the file contains. For example '.jpg' is a JPEG image and '.txt' is a text file.

FAT32 – File Allocation Table 32, the 32-bit file system available since Windows 95, which supports hard disks of up to 2 terabytes in size.

File extension – indicates to you and the operating system the type of file. The response when the file is opened varies depending on the application with which it is associated. Windows will prompt the user to select an action when unrecognised files are accessed.

Filter – a specific pattern or attribute that sorts data based on the parameters given. Think of it like digitally sifting flour, it removes the lumps and only gives you exactly what you want!

Firewall – a barrier between the internet and your computer. It protects you from outside threats like viruses and hackers by filtering the incoming data, blocking any potentially harmful information. Firewalls are an absolutely vital part of any system connected to the internet.

Floppy drive – or FDD, is used to read 3.5" magnetic media. These disks hold just 1.44 MB so are quickly becoming outdated. Older floppy drives used 5.25" disks.

Folders – also called directories, are what Windows uses to organise all the files. Think of them like the filing cabinets in an office, a way of keeping relevant files grouped together for easy access.

Freeware – free software. Some have 'Pro' features that are unlocked by paying a registration fee.

FTP – File Transfer Protocol, a method for downloading and uploading files to another system over a network. If you're creating a webpage you will usually have to login via FTP to upload the files.

GIF – Graphics Interchange Format, pronounced 'giff', commonly used on the web for images because it can be compressed, but not often for photos as it has limited color depth compared to JPG.

Graphics card – provides specialised graphics acceleration, allowing for advanced visuals and effects. Using a dedicated card rather than an onboard graphics solution takes pressure off the CPU.

Hard disk drive – the primary storage medium for PCs. They are a non-volatile type of memory.

Heatsink – used to transfer heat away from components and are often used in conjunction with fans. They're required for CPUs and most modern graphics cards, which run at extremely high temperatures.

HTTP – HyperText Transfer Protocol, the system used to display web pages. This tells a server that you're visiting to view a website. Sites beginning with www do not have to be prefixed with HTTP but those without, for example images.google.com, must have HTTP placed in front.

Icon – graphical representation of a file or other object. They usually indicate what type of file the item is but can be customised by the user.

IDE – Intelligent Drive Electronics or Integrated Drive Electronics, an interface used on CD/DVD drives and hard disks, where the controlling electronics are on the device itself. Sometimes referred to as EIDE, ATA or PATA.

ID3 tag – part of every MP3 is given over to holding data about the track, like title, artist, year and genre. This is the ID3 tag. It's used by MP3 players, hardware and software, to display information about a file.

Instant Messaging – a method of communication that creates a private chat room between yourself and at least one other person. Instant Messaging can be used to send text or files.

Intel – the largest manufacturer of central processing units in the world. The US giant had a monopoly on the CPU market until AMD introduced the Athlon series processor.

Java – a programming language created by Sun Microsystems and widely used in websites for features like chat rooms and games, through small Java programs called Applets. Also common on mobile phones.

Javascript – not related to Java, a scripting language created by Netscape for the production of interactive websites. It is supported by most modern web browsers.

JPG – popular image format, its full name is JPEG or Joint Photographic Expert Group. Often used for photos.

Jumpers – a circuit bridge that allows the user to adjust the settings of a device by covering the jumper pins with a plastic plug.

Kbps – Kilobits per second, used in reference to audio files to measure the quality of a track. 128kbps is considered CD quality but music fans claim they can hear the difference and prefer songs to be encoded as high as possible. As you increase the kbps the file size also gets larger.

LAME – an open-source MP3 encoder. The name was originally an acronym for Lame Ain't an MP3 Encoder. LAME is commonly thought to have the best sound quality of any MP3 encoder.

License agreement – the legalese that appears whenever you install software and lays out exactly what you can and can't do with an application. For the average home user there's probably not much of relevance or interest, if you're planning on using a program in a business capacity however you might want to have a read as some free applications require business users to purchase a license.

Live updates – allow a program to download new versions of itself or, in the case of spyware and antivirus tools, new information about threats to keep your system protected. Generally, live updates should be done in the background without requiring any user intervention.

Module – a program may be constructed from several linked modules, which provide different functions and are themselves small applications.

Motherboard – like the central nervous system of your PC, the other components all connect to the motherboard which then shunts data to the correct location.

MP3 – MPEG audio layer 3, the most popular digital audio format thanks to its ability to compress audio tracks to a fraction of their size without losing too much of the quality.

MSN passport – Microsoft's intended 'universal password' system, the idea being that you had one login and password that gave you access to instant messaging, email and websites. It didn't catch on quite as well as they'd hoped however, and has now mostly been discontinued, though Passport accounts still work to access Hotmail, MSN Messenger and other Microsoft services.

Network Places – a central location in Windows that shows your networked drives and computers.

NTFS – NT File System, used by Windows NT and later, NTFS offers several advantages over FAT32 such as greater reliability and file and folder security.

Open source software – applications where the source code can not only be downloaded but also freely modified, so if you've got the skills you can create your own version of the program.

Optical drive – used to read and write to CDs and DVDs. All new DVD drives can read and write both CDs and DVDs. Older drives may be read-only or capable of handling a particular type of DVD.

Partition – to divide a hard disk into several individual parts. The operating system then sees each drive partition as a separate disk, as if you had multiple physical hard disks installed.

Patch – software updates that fix holes or introduce new features into a program.

PCI – Peripheral Component Interconnect, the most common type of interface found on PC systems now, it still appears on the very latest PCI-express boards to support expansion hardware like sound cards, which have yet to switch to using PCI-express.

PCI-Express – the 'sequel' to PCI and AGP interfaces, PCI-express offers a (potentially) huge increase in bandwidth. Newer motherboards include one or two PCI-e slots specifically for graphics cards and several more for additional expansion cards, alongside a couple of standard PCI slots.

Phishing – a con using fake email and websites that tricks victims into entering sensitive details of online banks and other services such as Paypal and Ebay. The emails often tell you that your account is going to expire and give a link to reactivate. Although the link looks genuine it is actually going to a totally different location set up by the scammers. Phishing mails can often be spotted by the abundance of spelling and grammar mistakes, but in any case banks and other sites will not ever ask you to enter your details via email.

Plugins – additional software applications that are called by a web browser when needed to perform a specific function. Common plugins include Flash, QuickTime and Shockwave.

POP – Post Office Protocol, the most common email protocol. The latest version, POP3, can both send and receive email.

Pop-up – a browser window that pops up uninvited, usually for advertising. Pop-ups can be extremely irritating and without a pop-up blocker your system can be flooded. There are also pop-unders, which appear underneath your browser.

POST – Power On Self-Test, the check that every computer runs when it first powers up, to ensure that all necessary hardware is present and correct.

Power supply unit – (PSU) regulates the power to your system. The output of a PSU is measured in watts and modern components are quite power-hungry, so it's recommended that you get a good 350-400W PSU depending on your needs.

Process – a program that's currently running. Some background programs are constantly running while you're in Windows.

Proxy server – sits between your computer and the server you're trying to access, so the proxy receives the data and sends it on to you. Proxies are often used as a method of anonymously browsing the internet, since the rest of the net sees the proxy details and not yours.

Quarantine – when referring to antivirus and spyware applications, quarantine is where all the nasty programs get dumped. A protected area of the hard disk, security tools hold infected files in quarantine so that you can examine them later or restore them if necessary without them causing damage to your system.

Quick Launch – a customisable shortcut bar that's enabled through the Start Menu properties. Applications will often place a shortcut here as well as on the desktop.

RAID – Redundant Array of Independent Disks, two or more hard disks configured in a way that allows them to work together. There are many different types of RAID configurations, but RAID 1 is very useful for backup since it mirrors the data from one disk to the other, meaning that whenever data is written on one an identical copy is placed on the mirrored drive. If one of the disks fails, you have an exact backup copy.

RAM – Random Access Memory, provides temporary storage for files that are in use. RAM is volatile memory and loses the data held when power is switched off. Windows and other software require large amounts of RAM to operate.

RAR – compressed files. WinZip cannot read RAR files so you must use the WinRAR program or another compatible application.

Rescue Disk – provides help in a computer emergency by booting up your system with a variety of diagnostic tools. Many programs offer the ability to create rescue disks, some of which allow you to scan for and clean viruses or restore your computer to a previous state.

Resolution – defines the clarity of an image. With monitors, the resolution describes the number of pixels on screen, so a 1280 × 1024 resolution means that there are 1024 lines of 1280, a total of 1,310720 pixels. The maximum resolution changes depending on the capabilities of the monitor. All new 17–19" LCD monitors are capable of anything up to 1280 × 1024, with larger monitors handling 1600 × 1200 and varying specifications for widescreen displays.

SATA – Serial Advanced Technology Attachment, introduced to replace the ageing IDE interface. In addition to offering significant speed increases over IDE, SATA uses smaller cables, which helps with cable management and airflow inside the case. You do not need to configure master/slave settings since each drive has its own cable and numbered socket on the motherboard.

Shared folder – one that's accessible to other users of the same computer or network.

Shareware – trial software that can be used until a certain expiry date, at which point you must pay to continue using it.

Shortcut – link to another location on your computer. If you want to run an application, they save you from navigating to the directory where that program is stored.

Spam – junk email, named after the food product or the famous Monty Python sketch, depending on who you ask. Spam has become a huge problem with billions of mails sent every year hawking anything from Viagra to dubious loan offers. Most, if not all, email providers should now have some level of spam filtering.

Spyware – applications that monitor your computer and return data about your activities to the people or person's who created them. Often combined with adware. Many spyware applications are malicious, intrusive and incredibly stubborn, proving extremely difficult to remove once they're into your system. In many cases, there's a thin line between spyware and virus.

Start menu – appears when you click the Start button on the Windows taskbar. It's a vital part of Windows, containing links to applications and various parts of the operating system such as the Control Panel.

Switch – command line switches are used to enable or disable options when running a program from the command line or Run dialog.

System tray – the area to the far right of the taskbar. It is often used by applications to display status icons, while some programs have the option to minimize to the system tray rather than the taskbar.

Taskbar – the bar at the bottom of the display in Windows that stretches from one side of the display to the other. Program icons are shown here allowing you to access any application running by clicking it on the taskbar.

Toolbars – groups of related options and tools, usually represented by icons. Toolbars can be floating in a program window or embedded into the top or side of an application window (sometimes called sidebars.) Sidebars are often customisable, giving users the option to disable them or add and remove icons.

UAC – User Account Control. A new security feature in Windows Vista that asks the user to enter a password to authorise an application.

User switching – an option in Windows that allows you to quickly switch from one user account to another without losing data.

VBR – Variable Bit Rate. If you encode an audio track using VBR, the encoder will vary the bit rate (and therefore quality), dropping it during quieter moments. This has the potential to produce audio files that sound the same but that are smaller than those produced with CBR. The drawback is that some audio players are unable to play them back.

Virus – software program created for the purpose of causing damage to the system it infects. Some viruses simply damage files, others take over the systems and allow them to be remotely controlled, turning them into 'zombies'. This can be dangerous, as there have been cases where zombie systems were used to store pornography and pirated software without the knowledge of the owner.

Volatile memory – like RAM, a storage medium that loses data when it no longer has power.

Windows Registry – a database that stores configuration data for Windows, for both hardware and software. You can edit the registry yourself using the RegEdit tool, which is accessed through the Run menu. You must be careful though as mistakes can cripple Windows.

Wizard – a simplified program interface that makes it easier for beginners to use the application. Although wizard modes often have fewer features available they're much quicker if you just want to run a basic task.

WMA – Windows Media Audio. Competing digital audio format developed by Microsoft. WMA can include DRM so is a popular format for online stores selling music downloads. Most players support WMA (though some can't read its DRM) but one notable exception is Apple's iPod range.

WMV – Windows Media Video. Digital video format developed by Microsoft.

WWW – World Wide Web, or simply web. Servers that support a method of formatting documents – websites. Invented by British computer scientist Tim Berners-Lee, the first website went live on 6 August 1991.

Xvid – an open-source video codec. Xvid has overtaken Divx recently as the format of choice for sending video over the internet.

Zip – the most popular data compression format. It was invented by programmer Phil Katz in the '80s for his company PKWARE. He also made the first zip file utility, PKZIP.

Troubleshooting guide

Multimedia

Maintenance

Security

New! Features

Microsoft Windows Vista

Microsoft Windows Vista has a brand new user interface that makes it easier and faster to use than earlier versions of Windows. Tasks such as opening and closing applications, searching for files and changing settings have been streamlined. New and improved programs have been developed to help you manage and store pictures, send and receive emails, browse the Internet, backup your data and stay secure. And the flexible new interface allows you to customise toolbars and optimise your working environment using Sidebars and Gadgets.

What's New?

The **New!** icon in the table of contents highlights the sections that have been significantly revised to demonstrate how tasks are carried out in the new Vista operating system. The following lists all the significantly revised and new sections and their location in the book.